# BREAKTHROUGHS & Bless You's

## 100 DAYS OF LIFE'S UNEXPECTED BOUNCE BACKS AND BLESSINGS

### A Devotional Journal

*Breakthroughs & Bless Yous: 100 Days of LIfe's Unexpected Bounce-Backs and Blessings*

©2022 by Kara Barker

Published in McKinney, Texas, by Takman Publishing, Inc.

Scripture quotations are taken from the Holy Bible, New International Version®, NIV®, New King James Version®, NKJV® New American Standard Bible®, NASB®, New Living Translation Bible®, Copyright © 1973, 1978, 1984 by Biblica, Inc.® Used by permission of Zondervan. All rights reserved worldwide. www.zondervan.com The "NIV" and New International Version" are trademarks registered in the United States Patent and Trademark Office by Biblica, Inc.®

Book cover designed by Lindsey Parks for Money Graphics, LLC
Photo credit: Jaren Collins for JCI Creatives

ISBN: 978-1-66786-358-0

# Hello, MaximizHer!

I believe every woman has a desire to be appreciated, heard, seen and valued. This I know for certain. Truth be told, it is something that was already embedded in us from our Creator. Ladies, we are daughters of the Most High and His beloved children. But because we have a tendency to get in our own way, we often don't feel special to God. For me, I have wrestled with anxiety, self-doubt, perfectionism and toxic thinking for years. It wasn't until I learned how to give it over to God and surrender it all to Him that my life changed for the better. Navigating life's many ups and downs can be a scary roller coaster ride if you don't have a connection to the Father through Jesus Christ. The world will make you think you can do life in isolation but that is so far from the truth. Life is meant to be enjoyed in community with others. This is the moment right now for you to put aside your brokenness, despair and shame because the Holy Spirit is your confidant and comforter during this 100 day journey of self-discovery and renewal.

This book was written with you in mind. It is my hope that during your time reading through this journal, you will build your confidence muscles that are needed to position you for your next breakthrough. You opening up this devotional journal is not by happenstance. This is a divine and destined appointment. Oddly, God has been trying to get your attention for quite some time. And the truth is, you were made for more and you were born for such a time as this. God longs for you to spend quality time with Him because He wants to awaken your purpose, give you hope for the future and allow you to experience His unconditional love. I am so honored that our paths crossed. Maybe for the first or the second time if you've read my first book *Hallelujahs and Hiccups, 100 Day Devotional Journal*.

This is a devotional full of short stories, personal testimonies and laughter. Each day is centered around three pillars:

**Scripture**– Our breakthroughs are anchored in God's word through scripture. And your spiritual growth is heightened when you read the word. You may see the different translations but they are all taken from the Holy Bible.

**Reflection**– Each day is designed to give you a chance to reflect and journal your thoughts in the designated adjacent page.

**Prayer**– God already knows you and knows the desires of your heart, so by including a daily prayer, I want you to pause and allow the prayer to serve as a prompt to help you create a daily rhythm of prayer and devotion.

Spiritual growth happens over time and with creating healthy habits. Allow this book to serve as a daily habit to help you move closer to your next breakthrough. There is greatness within you. This is your season for becoming the best version of you. It's time to claim your next Breakthrough and Bless Yous!

# DAY 1
## Today is Your Day

For if you remain silent at this time, relief and deliverance for the Jews will arise from another place, but you and your father's family will perish. And who knows but that you have come to your royal position for such a time as this?

**— ESTHER 4:14 NIV**

Today is your day and you have all the potential in the world. You have been chosen for a reason and you should not forget it. You are brave, resilient and so deserving of good things. There is a story in the Bible that reminds me of this truth. The book of Esther. I love Esther! Esther found herself smack dab in the middle of political upheaval, cultural divides, and family drama to say the least. When faced with a royal decree that would annihilate her people, Esther had to make some tough choices. Would she remain silent or would she speak up? Would she blend in or would she stand out? Would she trust that God could use her to save a nation or would she cower in fear? Like Esther, you may be staring at a seemingly impossible situation. And what's true for Esther is true for you. Deliverance will come. God will give us victory. He will rescue His people. He will right the wrongs of this world. The question is not, will God prevail? The question is, will you be a part of the team? Jesus! Ok is it too early in the book to be shouting? Well, you and I, like Queen Esther, can act in a way that will bless more people than you could imagine. Why? Because today is your day! Today is the day that you take this opportunity to join God in His work. You don't need to become undone by tough times. You can become unleashed by our triumphant God. You, my friend, were made for this moment. Today is your day! Never doubt that. I believe in you. It all begins with your thinking. Keep your heart open to dreams. For as long as there's a dream, there is hope, and as long as there is hope, there is joy in living. So buckle up buttercup. Today is the day you start something new.

. . . . . . . . . . . . . . . . . . . . . . . . . . . . . . . . . . . . . . . . . . . . . . . . . . . . . . . . . . .

. . . . . . . . . . . . . . . . . . . . . . . . . . . . . . . . . . . . . . . . . . . . . . . . . . . . . . . . . . .

. . . . . . . . . . . . . . . . . . . . . . . . . . . . . . . . . . . . . . . . . . . . . . . . . . . . . . . . . . .

. . . . . . . . . . . . . . . . . . . . . . . . . . . . . . . . . . . . . . . . . . . . . . . . . . . . . . . . . . .

. . . . . . . . . . . . . . . . . . . . . . . . . . . . . . . . . . . . . . . . . . . . . . . . . . . . . . . . . . .

. . . . . . . . . . . . . . . . . . . . . . . . . . . . . . . . . . . . . . . . . . . . . . . . . . . . . . . . . . .

. . . . . . . . . . . . . . . . . . . . . . . . . . . . . . . . . . . . . . . . . . . . . . . . . . . . . . . . . . .

## Prayer for Today

Father in heaven, I receive new seasons of increase into my life by faith today. I choose to stand and declare Your promises because I know You have good things in store for my future. I bless You and thank You for another day to sing Your praises. In Jesus' Name. Amen.

# Mountain Climber

Whoever isolates himself seeks his own desire; he breaks out against all sound judgment.
— **PROVERBS 18:1 ESV**

Climbing up is always harder than coming down. I always wonder why some people get excited when they are faced with a mountain of adversity or any particular challenge and face obstacles head on. But there are some people who shy away from challenges and obstacles because the fear of failure can be paralyzing. There have been many opportunities that have passed me because I was determined to climb the mountain in front of me when it really wasn't my mountain to climb. There were times I knew the mountain was my opportunity and it was my moment so I went all in. I laced up my shoes, went full speed ahead and started hitting each level. But any good mountain climber knows you can't begin climbing Mt. Everest just by making the decision to climb it. You have to mentally and physically prepare for such an enormous task. Climbing mountains isn't like too many other adventure sports, even aside from the risk factors involved. Sure, the fitness requirements are somewhat similar to other activities (such as strength and stamina) but with mountain climbing, the higher you get, the harder your body has to work. Unfortunately, the only way that most of us can increase our efficiency at a higher altitude is to actually train at a higher altitude, which may not be an easy option. Not too long ago I finally came to the realization that there are some mountains that you and I were never meant to take on in our own strength. When your body works hard, your mind is working just as hard and maybe even harder. So regardless how hard you have trained physically, if your mindset is not in the right headspace you will fail. But don't fret. You don't have to make this climb solo because we were created to be in community but we also need community. When you are climbing to new altitudes you will see how there is safety in having a community of believers surrounding you in encouragement and prayer. I'm excited for you. While God is taking you to the next level, you must let go of the old for the new. All things considered, are you willing to do that?

. . . . . . . . . . . . . . . . . . . . . . . . . . . . . . . . . . . . . . . . . . . . .

. . . . . . . . . . . . . . . . . . . . . . . . . . . . . . . . . . . . . . . . . . . . .

. . . . . . . . . . . . . . . . . . . . . . . . . . . . . . . . . . . . . . . . . . . . .

. . . . . . . . . . . . . . . . . . . . . . . . . . . . . . . . . . . . . . . . . . . . .

. . . . . . . . . . . . . . . . . . . . . . . . . . . . . . . . . . . . . . . . . . . . .

. . . . . . . . . . . . . . . . . . . . . . . . . . . . . . . . . . . . . . . . . . . . .

. . . . . . . . . . . . . . . . . . . . . . . . . . . . . . . . . . . . . . . . . . . . .

## Prayer for Today

Holy Lord, thank You for grace. Please help me move beyond the obstacles that trip me up. Give me the strength and wisdom to look up and see the hope I run toward in Christ. Guide me Lord and allow me to lean and trust fully in You. With full surrender, I seek Your grace and mercy. In Jesus' name, Amen.

# Don't Dim Your Shine

*In the same way, let your light shine before others, so that they may see your good works and give glory to your Father who is in heaven.*
**— MATTHEW 5:16 ESV**

Truth be told, there are many times when I forget who I am and I tend to compare myself against the world's expectations and standards. In those doubting moments, my inner sabotager (yes we all know her) becomes much louder and boisterous than my outer boss lady's voice. Our inner voice is often fueled by insecurities and fears. However, if you allow your inner voice to overtake you, you will begin to shrink and play small. It doesn't benefit anyone when you shrink and play small. And when you play small you may be out of alignment with God's course for your life.

Hey, don't get all gloomy with me sis because you were birthed into this world for a reason not just for the obvious but to shine and glow because of God's faithfulness, goodness and mercy. If you don't retain any of the words that you are reading right now, remember this, we all were created with a little shine and sparkle. Do not allow any haters or naysayers to extinguish your spark. When you allow them to cause your light to dim or even if you dim it yourself, you're not only playing small but you're limiting your true greatness and God's designed purpose in your life. Your greatness is the gifts you have that people love about you. And yes there are many of them too! They are the things you're naturally gifted at and enjoy doing. Your greatness is being your most authentic self, the superhero that you have inside you. It's the best version of yourself as a human being, friend, family member, neighbor and leader. God put seeds of greatness on the inside of you. And those seeds are ready to germinate and blossom. I need you to be great and shine because the whole world needs a little shimmer and glimmer of the Holy Spirit. So shine on sis, shine on!

. . . . . . . . . . . . . . . . . . . . . . . . . . . . . . . . . . . . . . . . . . . . . . . . . . . . .

. . . . . . . . . . . . . . . . . . . . . . . . . . . . . . . . . . . . . . . . . . . . . . . . . . . . .

. . . . . . . . . . . . . . . . . . . . . . . . . . . . . . . . . . . . . . . . . . . . . . . . . . . . .

. . . . . . . . . . . . . . . . . . . . . . . . . . . . . . . . . . . . . . . . . . . . . . . . . . . . .

. . . . . . . . . . . . . . . . . . . . . . . . . . . . . . . . . . . . . . . . . . . . . . . . . . . . .

. . . . . . . . . . . . . . . . . . . . . . . . . . . . . . . . . . . . . . . . . . . . . . . . . . . . .

. . . . . . . . . . . . . . . . . . . . . . . . . . . . . . . . . . . . . . . . . . . . . . . . . . . . .

## Prayer for Today:

Lord, I pray for courage to walk in the plans that you have for me. I pray that you will keep me close as I step out in faith and do your will for my life. I admit I am afraid, but I will not let fear rob me from the blessings that will dim my shine. Heavenly Father, help me remain bold and confident in Jesus' name, Amen.

# DAY 4
## Peace Restored

The Lord is my Shepherd, I shall not want. He makes me lie down in green pastures; he leads me besides still waters; he restores my soul.
— **PSALM 23: 1-3 NRSV**

The world wants you to believe that what is most important is taking care of yourself. It says that your self-care is all up to you, and to feel better in life you just need to get away, get a manicure, get a massage, or take a trip to the shopping mall for retail therapy. Though these things are not bad, they fall short, as most of our attempts at self-care will. Maybe your day has just started and your thoughts are already beginning to spiral out of control or perhaps it's the middle of the night and you're struggling to find rest. Whatever season of difficulty you're facing, the enemy is attacking your peace of mind. In those overwhelming moments, as your mind fills with fear and anxiety, the best place to turn for comfort is an intimate relationship with God. We are not meant to control and fix everything that worries us. We were created to rest in God's love. I encourage you to take an alternate route and not solely shift to outward care but to look at God as the premium giver of self-care. Turning to God is the only true self-gift I have discovered that will truly heal and refresh my spirit. Jesus is the only one that can bring you to waters that will make you never thirst again and provide you bread to address your hunger. Just think about this, you've already chosen to let God care for you by picking up this journal. It shows that you place a priority on getting into the word. When you incorporate the word of God and prayer into your self-care routine, your peace will be restored. So as you go get your manicure or pedicure, bring this journal with you or better yet bring the good book with you and read some Psalms. There is no reason why you can't incorporate some spiritual enhancements to your self-care regimen. Friend, I don't know what you are going through today, what doubts you have or what questions you are seeking answers for. But I know God is with you and cares about your every need. And He alone is able to meet you and your needs right where you are. He's there when you need peace restored. Will you trust Him? As you put your trust in Him, He will restore your peace.

· · · · · · · · · · · · · · · · · · · · · · · · · · · · · · · · · · · · · · · · · · · ·

· · · · · · · · · · · · · · · · · · · · · · · · · · · · · · · · · · · · · · · · · · · ·

· · · · · · · · · · · · · · · · · · · · · · · · · · · · · · · · · · · · · · · · · · · ·

· · · · · · · · · · · · · · · · · · · · · · · · · · · · · · · · · · · · · · · · · · · ·

· · · · · · · · · · · · · · · · · · · · · · · · · · · · · · · · · · · · · · · · · · · ·

· · · · · · · · · · · · · · · · · · · · · · · · · · · · · · · · · · · · · · · · · · · ·

· · · · · · · · · · · · · · · · · · · · · · · · · · · · · · · · · · · · · · · · · · · ·

## Prayer for Today

Lord, I thank You for placing Your wonderful, powerful, protective peace in my life. I am grateful that You have positioned it to stand at the entrance of my heart and mind and that it dominates my mind and controls my life. Because what is inside me is what rules me, I choose to let this peace rise up and conquer me. With this peace standing at the gate of my heart and mind, I know it will disable the devil's ability to attack my emotions and will not permit his lies and accusations to slip into my mind. Thank You for loving me enough to put this powerful peace in my life. I pray this in Jesus' name!

# DAY 5
## Bigger Plans

*For I know the plans I have for you,' declares the Lord, 'plans to prosper you and not to harm you, plans to give you a hope and a future.*
**— JEREMIAH 29:11 NIV**

No matter where you are from, how old or young you are, when you got saved, or whether or not you have read through The One Year Bible, God has incredible plans for your life. The depth of your past is an indication of the height of your future. Your past does not define you. Isn't it good to know that God is working behind the scenes in your life, today? No matter what you may be facing, no matter what trial you may be going through, God has a plan to turn things around in your favor. You are called according to His purpose. So right now, He is working out a plan for your good. Right now, He is orchestrating the right people to come across your path. In other words, if you've been through a lot of negative things in the past, it just means that your future is bigger and brighter and greater than you can even imagine. The issue isn't even how big or small the dream is. That's up to God. That alliance is keeping you from your blessing. Dream her and then become her! Why not start today to embrace the woman you've always aspired to be. Become the woman that your childhood self needed. Become the woman that God intended you to become.

. . . . . . . . . . . . . . . . . . . . . . . . . . . . . . . . . . . . . . . . . . . . . . . . . .

. . . . . . . . . . . . . . . . . . . . . . . . . . . . . . . . . . . . . . . . . . . . . . . . . .

. . . . . . . . . . . . . . . . . . . . . . . . . . . . . . . . . . . . . . . . . . . . . . . . . .

. . . . . . . . . . . . . . . . . . . . . . . . . . . . . . . . . . . . . . . . . . . . . . . . . .

. . . . . . . . . . . . . . . . . . . . . . . . . . . . . . . . . . . . . . . . . . . . . . . . . .

. . . . . . . . . . . . . . . . . . . . . . . . . . . . . . . . . . . . . . . . . . . . . . . . . .

## Prayer for Today

Heavenly Father, thank You for always seeing me and my needs. Your word tells me that when I ask, it will be given to me and what I seek, I will find it. For when I ask of You, I must believe that I will receive it. What I seek shall be found. When I knock, You answer. So Father I praise You for being the door that is always opened; thank You Father, Amen.

# DAY 6
## The Prodigal Spirit

"...being strengthened with all power, according to his glorious might, for all endurance and patience with joy;"
— **COLOSSIANS 1:11 ESV**

Ladies, let's be honest. There's a prodigal in all of us. We all know the story about the prodigal son that had everything but left home seeking something better. He encountered some setbacks and serious challenges because of his stubbornness and disobedience but the turning point of the story was when he returned home and his father had open arms, clean clothing and food for him. There weren't any questions asked by the father and their relationship was restored. While writing this journal, my daughters moved out of the house to find their own way. To be honest, it was not my choice and the decision was not supported by my husband nor myself. However, we all have to grow and learn through the process and sometimes it takes learning to love through a mess to get to the miracle. The miracle in the prodigal son's story was the father having open arms and a welcoming posture for him returning home. We all have our prodigal moments when we go about our life without direction or intent and we just wander without seeking the Lord for help. You have wandered long enough. God is calling you home, daughter. No more running and chasing self-centered dreams. It's time to get off at the next exit and head back home. The main door to the house is unlocked and the alarm is off. Welcome back home.

. . . . . . . . . . . . . . . . . . . . . . . . . . . . . . . . . . . . . . . . . . . . . . . . . . . . . . . . . . . . . . .

. . . . . . . . . . . . . . . . . . . . . . . . . . . . . . . . . . . . . . . . . . . . . . . . . . . . . . . . . . . . . . .

. . . . . . . . . . . . . . . . . . . . . . . . . . . . . . . . . . . . . . . . . . . . . . . . . . . . . . . . . . . . . . .

. . . . . . . . . . . . . . . . . . . . . . . . . . . . . . . . . . . . . . . . . . . . . . . . . . . . . . . . . . . . . . .

. . . . . . . . . . . . . . . . . . . . . . . . . . . . . . . . . . . . . . . . . . . . . . . . . . . . . . . . . . . . . . .

. . . . . . . . . . . . . . . . . . . . . . . . . . . . . . . . . . . . . . . . . . . . . . . . . . . . . . . . . . . . . . .

. . . . . . . . . . . . . . . . . . . . . . . . . . . . . . . . . . . . . . . . . . . . . . . . . . . . . . . . . . . . . . .

## *Prayer for Today*

Father, thank You for loving me and showing me how to love myself even when I have prodigal moments. Help me become a better person. Lord protect those that have left home on bad terms. Restore and heal broken relationships. In Jesus' name, Amen.

# Don't Worry Be Happy

"Therefore do not worry about tomorrow, for tomorrow will worry about itself. Each day has enough trouble of its own."
— **MATTHEW 6:34 NIV**

You know what's more stressful than anything? Talking about how busy, stressed and unhappy you are. It starts with, "I'm not happy with my job." "I'm not happy with my body." "I'm not happy with my life." It seems that at some point in our lives, we each struggle with unhappiness, a spirit of discontentment and always wanting more. I remember a year ago being frustrated as I sat in my comfy living room chair, Bible open, listening to the Lord. Well, maybe it was more like talking to Him, telling Him what I wanted. What I wanted was to be promoted on my job, experience full restoration in my household and wanting to feel like I was adding value to the world. I thought if God would just give me the desires of my heart, I knew I could be happy. That's when this thought came to me: "Be happy now." If you don't learn to be happy while you're waiting for what you want, you'll never be happy when you finally get what you want.

To be frank, happiness cannot be the sole aim of our existence. Living out one's purpose by serving and loving others as Christ does should be the ultimate goal. When I stopped focusing so much on my wants and focused on what God wanted to do in and through me, contentment began to show up. In fact, happiness is an external indication of internal contentment. When Paul wrote in the book of Philippians, the word he used in exchange for happiness was "content" which actually means to find contentment or joy in one's path in life. Friend, we can spend so much energy pushing against our reality when life doesn't turn out the way we planned it. But resisting what is and trying to control what is beyond our control will lead you to an intersection called Anxiety Drive and Worry Place. You can expect that the next street over will be Frustration Lane and Anger Circle. So instead of taking a direction that will lead you to a dead-end, take an alternative path that begins with shifting your mindset and fully acknowledging your present circumstances with anticipation and hope. I know it might seem a little scary or difficult at first but truly accepting where you are will help you see the good and grace of God surrounding you. Because whatever is surrounding you today, God is surrounding it!

. . . . . . . . . . . . . . . . . . . . . . . . . . . . . . . . . . . . . . . . . . . . . . . . . . . . . . . . .

. . . . . . . . . . . . . . . . . . . . . . . . . . . . . . . . . . . . . . . . . . . . . . . . . . . . . . . . .

. . . . . . . . . . . . . . . . . . . . . . . . . . . . . . . . . . . . . . . . . . . . . . . . . . . . . . . . .

. . . . . . . . . . . . . . . . . . . . . . . . . . . . . . . . . . . . . . . . . . . . . . . . . . . . . . . . .

. . . . . . . . . . . . . . . . . . . . . . . . . . . . . . . . . . . . . . . . . . . . . . . . . . . . . . . . .

. . . . . . . . . . . . . . . . . . . . . . . . . . . . . . . . . . . . . . . . . . . . . . . . . . . . . . . . .

. . . . . . . . . . . . . . . . . . . . . . . . . . . . . . . . . . . . . . . . . . . . . . . . . . . . . . . . .

## Prayer for Today

Lord, help me embrace what is and live each day with thankfulness for the life I've been given. Give me the grace to be happy while I wait for what I want rather than insisting that I cannot be happy until I attain it. In Jesus' name, Amen.

# New Keys New Doors

"For I know the plans I have for you," declares the Lord, plans to prosper you and not to harm you, plans to give you hope and a future.
**— JEREMIAH 29:11 NIV**

Are you disappointed because a door has closed in your life? Did you expect something to come to pass only to discover that it didn't and now you're feeling let down? Have you ever prayed for something specific, released it over to God and just walked away? There is a saying that says, "new keys open new doors." I can attest to that. Some blessings can't be unlocked until you let go of old habits, old ways, bad company that doesn't mean you any good, destructive thinking and faithless actions. We serve a God who opens doors and when He opens a door no devil in hell can shut it and when He closes a door, no devil in hell can open it. In life there are many things we can be unsure about but God's love is not one of them. Nothing is unintentional with God. It wouldn't do any good for God or you if you weren't ready for a door that God opened for you. I believe that God is continually setting us up for the next chapter of our lives. He is going to open every opportunity and every door until we arrive at our last goal in paradise. So don't lose faith. On the off chance that you are searching for God to open a new door in your life, at that point, try looking at the things throughout your life that He is attempting to make better. Regardless of whether it is relationship building abilities, managing your income better, or building yourself more spiritually; consume yourself with your work and let God set you up for the next door of opportunity in your life.

But you might be asking what is an open door? An open door can be defined as doors of opportunities that lead to your success. The bible said the path of the just is like a shining light, that means the path of every child of God is full of open doors of great opportunities. In Jeremiah 29:11, He said He has a plan of a great future for us His children. This shows that every child of God is ordained to have a bright future. There is no limit to what God can do in your life. God wants to bless you, and He wants to increase you. Keep persisting. So today, I want you to do something different. Just try trusting in God even if you can't understand what's going on right now in your life. Just seek Him and He will shed a light that will lead and show you the way to the open door. He is there for you; lovingly waiting, caring, knocking and His arm is extended out with an open hand to grab yours to guide you to your next door. He will meet you where you are, today.

· · · · · · · · · · · · · · · · · · · · · · · · · · · · · · · · · · · · · · · · · · · · ·

· · · · · · · · · · · · · · · · · · · · · · · · · · · · · · · · · · · · · · · · · · · · ·

· · · · · · · · · · · · · · · · · · · · · · · · · · · · · · · · · · · · · · · · · · · · ·

· · · · · · · · · · · · · · · · · · · · · · · · · · · · · · · · · · · · · · · · · · · · ·

· · · · · · · · · · · · · · · · · · · · · · · · · · · · · · · · · · · · · · · · · · · · ·

· · · · · · · · · · · · · · · · · · · · · · · · · · · · · · · · · · · · · · · · · · · · ·

· · · · · · · · · · · · · · · · · · · · · · · · · · · · · · · · · · · · · · · · · · · · ·

## Prayer for Today

Dear Lord, I thank You for who You are and for Your divine power. I pray that just as You sent Your angel to open up the gates of the prison for Paul, You will open up doors in my life. I pray that You open the heavens so that I can receive my breakthrough here on earth. I thank You for opening new doors for me and letting heaven reign down on me, Amen.

# Too Blessed to be Stressed

Abide in me, and I in you. As the branch cannot bear fruit of itself, except it abides in the vine; so neither can ye, except ye abide in me.

**— JOHN 15:4 ASV**

There's no shortage of worry these days. Just because you're busy doesn't mean you're productive. Being busy is fueled by perfectionism while being productive is fueled by purpose. Whether you're a mom pulled in five different directions, a student stressed over your next exam or a dad wondering where your next job will come from, we all will experience stress and worry during the course of our lives. As a matter of fact, as I am writing this book I am feeling a little overwhelmed and stretched because I am behind schedule writing this book and just received news that I will be moving into a new role within my organization for a leadership developmental assignment. Several years ago, I felt like I had a ton of bricks stacked on my back and I was thrown into the deep sea and was sinking. At that very moment, I felt like God had left the building and I was left in complete chaos. I was operating way out of my lane and trying to recreate my own plan without consulting the Master Architect, God. I've learned the hard way that constantly working like a crazy woman without rest does not necessarily result in productivity. In fact, it can have the opposite effect. Believe me, I've been there. It all started in 2018. I wasn't on speaking terms with my daughters, my marriage was strained because of differing parenting styles and I was being passed over or should I say left behind when it came to career advancement. It was the summer of July 2020, when my body literally gave out and I was subsequently diagnosed with shingles and borderline high blood pressure. As if the shingles weren't bad enough!

Do you know that stress will rob you of your joy, dismantle your peace and deny you hope for the present as well as the future? Let me say it another way, stress is like the repo man. It comes by forcefully entering your world and wrecking it while you try to hold on to the little joy you have left. However, here is some good news, stress may come in and create havoc but you don't have to allow it to hijack your future. So keeping it real, yes, beloved you will experience stress but you can manage it and keep it confined to its place. So let's make a commitment today. When you find yourself stressed, connect with a friend, family member, counselor or even your pastor to help you regain your confidence and regain your balanced mindset. Truth be told, you were not created to be an anxious, stressed out woman with no hope nor joy but a woman who when plugged in to the source of the Holy Spirit, you will discover a continuous supply of peace, love and longsuffering.

· · · · · · · · · · · · · · · · · · · · · · · · · · · · · · · · · · · · · · · · · · · · · · · ·

· · · · · · · · · · · · · · · · · · · · · · · · · · · · · · · · · · · · · · · · · · · · · · · ·

· · · · · · · · · · · · · · · · · · · · · · · · · · · · · · · · · · · · · · · · · · · · · · · ·

· · · · · · · · · · · · · · · · · · · · · · · · · · · · · · · · · · · · · · · · · · · · · · · ·

· · · · · · · · · · · · · · · · · · · · · · · · · · · · · · · · · · · · · · · · · · · · · · · ·

· · · · · · · · · · · · · · · · · · · · · · · · · · · · · · · · · · · · · · · · · · · · · · · ·

· · · · · · · · · · · · · · · · · · · · · · · · · · · · · · · · · · · · · · · · · · · · · · · ·

## *Prayer for Today*

Lord, help me lean in more and be fully submitted to You. Let Your Holy Spirit guide me and lead me in the direction I should go, in Jesus' name, Amen.

# CTRL + ALT + DELETE

Look to the Lord and his strength; seek his face always.
## — 1 CHRONICLES 16:11 NIV

Did you know that when you're using a computer, with a Windows operating system, when you select the combination, CTRL + ALT + DELETE, you can terminate any task which can lead to a system reboot? There are times when that keystroke will not suffice, and you need to do a hard reset or power off. Think about how this relates to our day to day grind when it often leads to feeling overwhelmed, stressed and frustrated and in those times, you don't just need a system or mind reboot you need a hard restart. Everyone hits a brick wall at some time in their life. Motivation dips, energy dries up and focus pretty much disappears. Professional development and personal growth stagnate and health may be neglected. Hitting a brick wall means we have come across or perceive ourselves to have come across an insurmountable obstacle. We become stuck or unmotivated. It could be that you have been carrying out a lengthy, time-consuming task at work and you cannot access relevant information to progress it any further; you are stuck. Perhaps you have been trying to resolve a conflict and sense you are not moving forward; you feel stuck. It may be that you are overworked, tired, bored, all of which can make you feel like you have hit a wall and cannot get past it. Does any of this sound familiar?

When you hit the wall, the first thing to do is simply stop. Whatever you're doing, just stop. If you're standing, sit down and lean back in your chair. Now breathe. When we're feeling a lot of pressure or anxiety, we tend to stop breathing. So just lean back for a few minutes and consciously focus on your breath coming in and going out. Inhale slowly, now exhale. If it's helpful, close your eyes. Take deep and full breaths, imagining that you're breathing into your chair or into the floor. Pause for a second or two after each exhalation to rest before you inhale again. This is your only job right now. Put all of your attention on breathing in and out, with brief pauses in between. That's all. Just breathe. But when your reboot aka "breathing" does not help you get back to center, I would encourage you to seek the manual of the main operating system, God's word. Ask God for divine intervention or a reset. God created a day to contain 24 hours and oftentimes we wonder why we can't get everything done. Have you considered that maybe you're unable to get things done because you're focusing on things throughout the day that God never intended you to focus on? If that's you, start today by taking an intentional pause and hit the CTRL + ALT + DELETE buttons to pause and stop your unhealthy practices and just seek the Heavenly Father.

· · · · · · · · · · · · · · · · · · · · · · · · · · · · · · · · · · · · · · · · · · · · · · ·

· · · · · · · · · · · · · · · · · · · · · · · · · · · · · · · · · · · · · · · · · · · · · · ·

· · · · · · · · · · · · · · · · · · · · · · · · · · · · · · · · · · · · · · · · · · · · · · ·

· · · · · · · · · · · · · · · · · · · · · · · · · · · · · · · · · · · · · · · · · · · · · · ·

· · · · · · · · · · · · · · · · · · · · · · · · · · · · · · · · · · · · · · · · · · · · · · ·

· · · · · · · · · · · · · · · · · · · · · · · · · · · · · · · · · · · · · · · · · · · · · · ·

· · · · · · · · · · · · · · · · · · · · · · · · · · · · · · · · · · · · · · · · · · · · · · ·

## *Prayer for Today:*

Heavenly Father, when things get particularly stressful. And when family, work, and fatigue all take their toll on me, please help me dwell and meditate on scriptures that remind me to let go and let God. In Jesus' name Amen.

# Take the Limits Off

*Now all glory to God, who is able, through his mighty power at work within us, to accomplish infinitely more than we might ask or think.*

**— EPHESIANS 3:20 NLT**

One of the most amazing yet challenging scriptures to me is Ephesians 3:20 that reads, "Now unto Him who is able to do exceedingly abundantly beyond all that we ask, think or imagine, according to the power that works in us, to Him be glory in the church and in Christ Jesus throughout all generations, forever and ever. Amen." In this scripture Paul is saying God's ability is beyond my ability to ask or even imagine what it could be like for His power to flow through me. Did you know that chances are, you have been limiting God? We don't intend to limit God but we often do by looking at ourselves thinking we are not anyone special or we are not smart enough, etc. When God sees you, He sees unlimited possibility. He sees unlimited potential. He sees unlimited resources. God's grace and favor in your life enables you to become what He sees. But first, you have to open your heart and take the limits off of your life. We all know about Isaac Newton's theory on gravity. What goes up, must come down. But there is also spiritual gravity. Spiritual gravity is what weighs us down in our soul. Are you weighed down by fear, insecurity, judgment, failures, etc.? We cannot let these things hold us down. Fear of failure is real. But a greater fear is to live your life playing it too safe. Choose today to take the limits off and put on God's word. Give weight to prayer. Give weight to the Holy Spirit. Accept the unique call of God on your life. Because when we take on God's weight, it is easy and light. It's time to WOMAN UP and remove the limitations today!

. . . . . . . . . . . . . . . . . . . . . . . . . . . . . . . . . . . . . . . . . . . . . . . . . . . . . .

. . . . . . . . . . . . . . . . . . . . . . . . . . . . . . . . . . . . . . . . . . . . . . . . . . . . . .

. . . . . . . . . . . . . . . . . . . . . . . . . . . . . . . . . . . . . . . . . . . . . . . . . . . . . .

. . . . . . . . . . . . . . . . . . . . . . . . . . . . . . . . . . . . . . . . . . . . . . . . . . . . . .

. . . . . . . . . . . . . . . . . . . . . . . . . . . . . . . . . . . . . . . . . . . . . . . . . . . . . .

. . . . . . . . . . . . . . . . . . . . . . . . . . . . . . . . . . . . . . . . . . . . . . . . . . . . . .

. . . . . . . . . . . . . . . . . . . . . . . . . . . . . . . . . . . . . . . . . . . . . . . . . . . . . .

## Prayer for Today

God, I am taking the limits off of You working in my life. I am excited to see what You will do with me. I am not going to sit here and die. I am going to start moving with whatever You show me to do next! In Jesus' name, Amen.

# DAY 12
## Fireproof Faith

He said, "Look! I see four men walking around in the fire, unbound and unharmed, and the fourth looks like a son of the gods."
### – DANIEL 3:25 NIV

We would love to believe that faith makes the problems of life disappear. How grand would it be if we could live our lives without hassle, discouragement or frustration? Sadly, we know this is not the case. We are never removed from the frailty of life. We go through times of burden, hardship, and struggle. There may even be seasons where we feel tossed into a fiery furnace of affliction. Shadrack, Meshack and Abednego knew about fiery afflictions, literally. These three young Hebrew men, probably no more than 20 years of age, find themselves on the wrong side of the King's ire. They are arrested and threatened with death, all because they would not violate their allegiance to God. In refusing to bow down before the golden statue, they opposed the royal edict and must suffer the consequences. What do you think they were feeling as they were hauled before the king? Do you think they were afraid? Do you think they felt overwhelmed, discouraged, or downcast? And what about when they were bound and brought to the furnace? The truth on which we stand is not that God shelters us from our struggles, but that God's love remains with us during those times of struggle. God is present within the flames. Our times of hardship and struggle speak not of God's absence. In fact, these are the times when God draws near. Shadrach, Meshack and Abednego weren't saved from entering the furnace. They were surrounded by the flames. It was in that oven, and not a moment before, that they met the presence of the one who appears like the son of God. God was in the midst of the fire. And because God was present, the flames had no power over them.

Fire will either burn you or purify you. True faith has actions with it. A lot of times people say they believe one way, but with their actions, they're doing just the opposite. We have to understand that faith will work in either direction. They talk about it and say, "It's going to be bad this year." They expect it and a few months later, they've got it. Their faith worked. But instead of making plans for the worst, why don't you make plans for the best?

You are not alone. Christ can enter your areas of despair and darkness and bring hope and healing. Friend, there is no place in our lives where Christ is not present. Jesus promises us; "Surely, I am with you to the very end of the age" Matthew 28:20. If you find yourself overwhelmed by struggles or stress, simply remember this truth. In fact, try inserting your name at the start of the verse as a way to hear this declaration spoken directly over you.

. . . . . . . . . . . . . . . . . . . . . . . . . . . . . . . . . . . . . . . . . . . . . . . . . . . . . . . . . . . . .

. . . . . . . . . . . . . . . . . . . . . . . . . . . . . . . . . . . . . . . . . . . . . . . . . . . . . . . . . . . . .

. . . . . . . . . . . . . . . . . . . . . . . . . . . . . . . . . . . . . . . . . . . . . . . . . . . . . . . . . . . . .

. . . . . . . . . . . . . . . . . . . . . . . . . . . . . . . . . . . . . . . . . . . . . . . . . . . . . . . . . . . . .

. . . . . . . . . . . . . . . . . . . . . . . . . . . . . . . . . . . . . . . . . . . . . . . . . . . . . . . . . . . . .

. . . . . . . . . . . . . . . . . . . . . . . . . . . . . . . . . . . . . . . . . . . . . . . . . . . . . . . . . . . . .

. . . . . . . . . . . . . . . . . . . . . . . . . . . . . . . . . . . . . . . . . . . . . . . . . . . . . . . . . . . . .

## Prayer for Today

Almighty God, when I feel overwhelmed by fiery furnaces, please open my eyes to see You are with me. Help me to feel the comforting balm of Your presence, as You uphold my life. I pray this in the name of Jesus, the one who comes to me and stands with me. In Jesus' name, Amen.

# Woman, Come Forth

*My thoughts are nothing like your thoughts, says the Lord. And my ways are far beyond anything you could imagine.*

**— ISAIAH 55:8 NLT**

Have you ever had an issue with God's timing? I have. I get anxious, afraid and start questioning if God is even aware of my feelings or circumstances. When you begin to think He is slow to answer (your timing) remember that He alone is sovereign and He knows what you need, who you need, how you need it and when you need it. This reminds me of the story of Lazarus. Even though Lazarus had been dead for several days, Jesus pulls Him back from death's grasp and restores him to life. All it took was one command for Jesus. Let me pause and say that again, all it took was one command from Jesus, just one. All you need is one move from God, one intervention from God, one redirection from God, one act of favor from God and He can take the things that were once dead, done and left behind and make those things alive again. That includes you! The voice that spoke creation into existence now calls Lazarus out of the darkness of death and into the light of life again. God's delays are not God's denials. Let me say that again so you can get that into your spirit, God's delays are not His denials. His timing may not always align with our timing. In this story of Lazarus, God knew exactly when He needed to show up and what He needed to do. However, one of the main reasons many of us become paralyzed and begin to operate in fear is that we've created limitations or restrictions on God, thinking that He can't handle the small things and that is far from the truth. If you've ever undermined your own progress or desires, you're not alone. It's something so many of us unconsciously do. Extraordinary people do what ordinary people do occasionally. If you were 100% sure that any action you took would succeed, what would you do? Think about it. Are you boldly going for it, or are you cautiously playing it safe?

Speaking from a person who is semi-risk averse, I get it. We have retirement plans, 401K's, we have reliable salaries. And for me I have all of that, making six figures but I am still playing it safe and small. Because it is easier that way and the path has less opposition. If we stayed in a role and maxed out our salaries, would we still be happy and would our lives have significance and value?

In reality, when we try to play it safe, we often settle for a lesser goal with a clear path. Someone once said, "Failure isn't the problem, low aim is." Ouch! Call 911, we have a woman down. Just think on this statement of settling and not moving forward. If you were confident you could not fail, there would be no hesitation between your initial bold thought and starting the actions that would make it real. But I know this is easier said than easy to do. But if we just stopped for a moment and operated from a mindset that was positioned and poised for action, the cost of failure would weigh far less than just moving forward.

Woman come forth and lace up your boots. Stand tall and start taking intentional steps toward your goals and aspirations. You have stayed in the valley too long. Whatever you think you can do, do it. If you have a choice between a bold course of action and a tentative, cautious one, choose the bold one. Boldness has power and purpose in it. As it states in Isaiah 55:8 and 9 "For my thoughts are not your thoughts, neither are your ways my ways,' declares the Lord. 'As the heavens are higher than the earth, so are my ways higher than your ways and my thoughts than your thoughts." Redirect your focus on trusting and leaning in on the word of God. God wants you to trust Him and to come forth. Remember that when God moves He not only moves for the short term experiences but He moves for longer term outcomes and results. When God appoints, He also anoints you to conquer the things that are set before you. So when He tells you to come forth, it's time to get ready, get back in position and just leap! Nothing is too big and no problem is too difficult for God to handle. Not even death itself.

. . . . . . . . . . . . . . . . . . . . . . . . . . . . . . . . . . . . . . . . . .

. . . . . . . . . . . . . . . . . . . . . . . . . . . . . . . . . . . . . . . . . .

. . . . . . . . . . . . . . . . . . . . . . . . . . . . . . . . . . . . . . . . . .

. . . . . . . . . . . . . . . . . . . . . . . . . . . . . . . . . . . . . . . . . .

. . . . . . . . . . . . . . . . . . . . . . . . . . . . . . . . . . . . . . . . . .

. . . . . . . . . . . . . . . . . . . . . . . . . . . . . . . . . . . . . . . . . .

. . . . . . . . . . . . . . . . . . . . . . . . . . . . . . . . . . . . . . . . . .

## Prayer for Today

O Lord my God, You know my every need. You have promised that You will give strength to the weary and increase the power of the weak. Please help me to draw on Your strength as I feel weak, to receive your healing when I feel pain and to know Your comfort in the midst of my distress. You are the God of endurance and encouragement. Help me to live in perfect harmony with You and glorify You with my thoughts, words and deeds. Through Jesus Christ, our Lord. Amen.

# It's Already Yours

You bless the righteous , O Lord; you cover them with favor as with a shield.
**— PSALM 5:12 NRSV**

The other day I received an email from an online store that said, "The item you ordered is now out of stock and unfortunately we don't know when it will be restocked." I was given the option of canceling my order or letting it stand and they would send me the item "whenever" they had it in stock again. Can you imagine if our relationship with God was like that? "God, I really need some extra grace today." "Oh sorry, I'm all out of grace for today. Please try again tomorrow. "Father, I need Your mercy!" "No mercy is available at this time. I don't know when it will be available again, but I'll keep you updated." "Lord, please give me wisdom in this situation." "I don't have any new wisdom to share right now. I'll have some next week so I'll send it to you then. In the meantime, try searching for some self-help videos or sermons or something." Aren't you glad God is not like that? Aren't you so thankful He's never "out of stock" and that He always has everything we need? Aren't you thrilled you don't even have to wait around for your request to be processed or your order to be shipped? And aren't you so grateful to know you'll never have to look elsewhere to find what you need because you are covered, you have favor and God's got your back? But favor can be viewed differently by many people. Some people think of favor as material prosperity or medical breakthroughs. Favor is not all about money and possessions; it is protection. We serve a very real and powerful God who will shield us from the enemy's attacks. But you must know that your strength alone it's not enough. You need the full armor of God for the battle you're facing and if you're not in a battle now, just hold on because it is coming. With God on your side you can rest and be encouraged that you will be safe in His arms. Know that you are covered and protected as you go into your day today because the victory is already yours in Jesus' name. Amen!

. . . . . . . . . . . . . . . . . . . . . . . . . . . . . . . . . . . . . . . . . . . . . . . . . . . . . . . . . . . . .

. . . . . . . . . . . . . . . . . . . . . . . . . . . . . . . . . . . . . . . . . . . . . . . . . . . . . . . . . . . . .

. . . . . . . . . . . . . . . . . . . . . . . . . . . . . . . . . . . . . . . . . . . . . . . . . . . . . . . . . . . . .

. . . . . . . . . . . . . . . . . . . . . . . . . . . . . . . . . . . . . . . . . . . . . . . . . . . . . . . . . . . . .

. . . . . . . . . . . . . . . . . . . . . . . . . . . . . . . . . . . . . . . . . . . . . . . . . . . . . . . . . . . . .

. . . . . . . . . . . . . . . . . . . . . . . . . . . . . . . . . . . . . . . . . . . . . . . . . . . . . . . . . . . . .

. . . . . . . . . . . . . . . . . . . . . . . . . . . . . . . . . . . . . . . . . . . . . . . . . . . . . . . . . . . . .

## Prayer for Today

Dear Jesus, I've stood right on the edge, waiting for You to choose someone else, or naming all the reasons I'm not qualified or equipped. Today I hear Your voice and I take that step, for You are with me. In Your name I pray, Amen.

# DAY 15
# Heartaches & Heartburn

"Create in me a pure heart, O God,
and renew a steadfast spirit within me."
**—PSALM 51:10 NIV**

No matter the preventive measures I take, it's inevitable that I will get heartburn if I eat anything spicy late at night and my heart will hurt if someone intentionally lets me down. Broken hearts come in all shapes and sizes, but not one goes unnoticed by Jesus. Hearts break at the end of a relationship, a broken friendship or the death of a loved one. Scripture tells us to guard our hearts, but if your heart is hurting, how do you heal it? Whether you're experiencing jealousy, injustice, loneliness or rejection, your brokenness isn't too much for Jesus to mend. When our hearts are broken, there is room for Jesus to work. A broken heart is an open heart. We don't have to be thankful when we are heartbroken, but we can be thankful for the One who mends our broken hearts with His ferocious love. Jesus' love for us is the greatest love story of all time. He loves us so much it hurts (literally). Jesus was pierced to a cross for our sins. He died so we could truly live. We were all once "broken" because we live in a broken world. But we have a Savior whose love never runs dry. People in our lives will come and go, but Jesus' is the only relationship that can't be taken away. He remains with us and in constant pursuit of us. When our identity is in Jesus, we don't have to be a slave to the way people have wronged us. We know our worth and identity come from Him so our hearts are free to respond with grace and love. Broken hearts can lead to blessings, including a deeper relationship with Jesus or a deeper knowledge of who He is. When I didn't get the job, I ran closer to God, when my kids left the house abruptly my heart hurt but I ran closer to God, when I went through infidelity in my marriage I had to run even faster to God. Beloved, we get to taste and see His goodness when our hearts are vulnerable in seeking Him. We get a glimpse of real love right here on Earth. Our hope is an everlasting hope in Jesus. I don't know what you have been through in your life, but I know this: God is faithful. He binds up wounds when we think we will never heal. He mends our hearts when we think they are too broken to mend. He offers His grace when life gives us so much more than we can handle alone. God is not done with your life. He can take what's broken and bruised and transform it into something beautiful.

. . . . . . . . . . . . . . . . . . . . . . . . . . . . . . . . . . . . . . . . . . . . . . . . . . . . . . . . . . . . . . . . . . . . . . . . .

. . . . . . . . . . . . . . . . . . . . . . . . . . . . . . . . . . . . . . . . . . . . . . . . . . . . . . . . . . . . . . . . . . . . . . . . .

. . . . . . . . . . . . . . . . . . . . . . . . . . . . . . . . . . . . . . . . . . . . . . . . . . . . . . . . . . . . . . . . . . . . . . . . .

. . . . . . . . . . . . . . . . . . . . . . . . . . . . . . . . . . . . . . . . . . . . . . . . . . . . . . . . . . . . . . . . . . . . . . . . .

. . . . . . . . . . . . . . . . . . . . . . . . . . . . . . . . . . . . . . . . . . . . . . . . . . . . . . . . . . . . . . . . . . . . . . . . .

. . . . . . . . . . . . . . . . . . . . . . . . . . . . . . . . . . . . . . . . . . . . . . . . . . . . . . . . . . . . . . . . . . . . . . . . .

. . . . . . . . . . . . . . . . . . . . . . . . . . . . . . . . . . . . . . . . . . . . . . . . . . . . . . . . . . . . . . . . . . . . . . . . .

## Prayer for Today

God, I pray that You heal my broken heart. Your word says that You will heal me completely and I surrender my broken heart to You to heal. You are the ultimate healer and I trust that You will heal my broken heart. Thank You for making me whole again. Amen

# Maybe God Is Tryin' To Tell You Somethin'

*The angel of the Lord said to her, "Return to your mistress, and submit to her authority."*
**GENESIS 16:9 NLT**

I'm not a fan of the movie The Color Purple. Maybe because of the physical and mental abuse. However, there were a few songs that I will always remember, and one of them was sung by the infamous character Shug Avery while she was singing in her father's church belting, "God is tryin' to tell you somethin'." Sis, it's time for you to seek God's power for your healing. You can't sit in this dark place forever. It's time to shift. It can start with that subtle feeling inside, leading you toward a path you never thought to travel. Maybe it's the small voice that whispers in your mind to think toward a different perspective than the one you have now. Or, it could be hearing a word from God that you think isn't possible, only to hear it confirmed over and over by others who had no knowledge of this message beforehand. When we are at a crossroad in life or just feel a stirring in our hearts for more than our present circumstances, this is usually when God might be telling us something we need to hear or do. God calls us to seek Him daily for answers, requests and peace that comes from obedience and trust in Him. When we make it a point to follow Him, He can open up more of the plan He has in store for each of us. So, if God is telling you to do something, your willingness to surrender will activate His intervention and blessings. God will answer your prayers when the time is right. Worrying doesn't take away tomorrow's troubles. It takes away today's peace. Anytime you don't have peace in your heart about something or feel uneasiness, that's a sign that you should stop and pray to make sure you are in line with God's plan for your life. Remember, His plans for you are good. He leads you by peace and fills you with His joy. Trust me, it will get better in due time. In today's reading I don't want you to miss this divine moment, because God is trying to tell you something right now. He is telling you to get back up, take the lead, speak up, shake the dirt off your shoes and start over again but this time with Him. Now is the right time to move with the authority and power of the Holy Spirit. Now is the time to tell the enemy you are done living this mundane life with no zeal and joy. God is trying to tell you something, you just need to pause and listen.

. . . . . . . . . . . . . . . . . . . . . . . . . . . . . . . . . . . . . . . . . . . . . . . . . . .

. . . . . . . . . . . . . . . . . . . . . . . . . . . . . . . . . . . . . . . . . . . . . . . . . . .

. . . . . . . . . . . . . . . . . . . . . . . . . . . . . . . . . . . . . . . . . . . . . . . . . . .

. . . . . . . . . . . . . . . . . . . . . . . . . . . . . . . . . . . . . . . . . . . . . . . . . . .

. . . . . . . . . . . . . . . . . . . . . . . . . . . . . . . . . . . . . . . . . . . . . . . . . . .

. . . . . . . . . . . . . . . . . . . . . . . . . . . . . . . . . . . . . . . . . . . . . . . . . . .

. . . . . . . . . . . . . . . . . . . . . . . . . . . . . . . . . . . . . . . . . . . . . . . . . . .

## Prayer for Today

God, thank you for all you've done for me throughout my life, even while You were knitting me inside my mother's womb. I can't thank You enough for all You have done for me, especially in sending Your Son Jesus to die on the cross for my sins. Lord, prepare my heart to follow Your call. Help me be alert and ready for when You call me to do something, go somewhere, or to change something about myself to shine my light for You. Lead me to where You need me most and I thank you for believing and loving me. In Jesus's name. Amen.

# DAY 17
## Amazingly You

Thank you for making me so wonderfully complex!
Your workmanship is marvelous—how well I know it.
**— PSALM 139:14 NLT**

*Pssst* . . . pull up a chair and I'll tell you a secret. You'd better lean in close for this one. Ready? You don't have to *do* more, *be* more, *have* more to be amazing. You have extraordinary potential in fulfilling your life with anything and everything that you want. But it isn't always easy and it takes hard work. It takes knowing who you are and planning where you want to go and being courageous enough to give your dreams and yourself a chance. Here's another secret: Truth is not just a fact we store in our heads. Truth is a Person we seek with our hearts. That's your cue to shout......Jesus! You're probably familiar with the lyrics of the well-known hymn "Amazing Grace." It's so hopeful to think of God's grace saving "a wretch like me." But for years I lived as though the lyrics were actually "God, help me be so amazing that I won't need grace!" It was as if I secretly hoped that, if I were amazing enough, I could avoid being the broken, messed-up wretch I knew I really was. It wasn't until I heard a minister's teaching on Jesus' Sermon on the Mount that I finally realized I could never be good enough. I could never jump high enough or perform well enough not to need God's grace.

I discovered that being amazing won't save you and this is actually really good news. Up until that discovery in my life, I spent a lot of time and energy trying to do the best and be the best. I struggled under the weight of expectation both internal and external, always striving to perform well. Whether it's how we present ourselves on social media platforms, what we want our church community to think about us, or what we do in our everyday interactions with friends and family, a pressure to do more creeps in. Before we know it, we've put our hope in being amazing ourselves rather than being amazed by God's grace that saves us from our wretchedness. We may have been wounded by lies, but we have not lost the battle. And we have been promised victory. We're going to defeat discouragement, banish fear, and break free from all that's been keeping us from embracing who we are and becoming all God created us to be. When you get the choice to sit it out or dance, I hope you dance. As the hymn tells us, His amazing grace accomplishes the impossible: It redeems us from sin, restores us to newness of life and makes us fit for God's holy presence forever. And when you have God in your life you're nothing short of just amazing! Psalm 139:14 declares, "I praise you because you made me in an amazing and wonderful way." In other words, recognizing the truth about who we are leads to praise not to pride. Honoring our Maker is the ultimate goal of what we're doing together. When we believe in God's amazing power, we can rest assured that all things are possible. Don't think that miracles and blessings don't exist. So know this, if God is in your life, you are amazing, sis! Don't let anyone tell you anything less.

. . . . . . . . . . . . . . . . . . . . . . . . . . . . . . . . . . . . . . . . . . . . . . . . . . . .

. . . . . . . . . . . . . . . . . . . . . . . . . . . . . . . . . . . . . . . . . . . . . . . . . . . .

. . . . . . . . . . . . . . . . . . . . . . . . . . . . . . . . . . . . . . . . . . . . . . . . . . . .

. . . . . . . . . . . . . . . . . . . . . . . . . . . . . . . . . . . . . . . . . . . . . . . . . . . .

. . . . . . . . . . . . . . . . . . . . . . . . . . . . . . . . . . . . . . . . . . . . . . . . . . . .

. . . . . . . . . . . . . . . . . . . . . . . . . . . . . . . . . . . . . . . . . . . . . . . . . . . .

## Prayer For Today

God, help me accept myself for who I am. Free me from my desire to copy others and please everyone else. I want to be a better me. Show me what's really mine. My faults, my virtues. Then mold me, oh Lord, shape me and make me confident as your child. And may it all manifest in acts of kindness, mercy and love. Let my life glorify You and bring more souls to your heavenly banquet. In Jesus name, Amen.

# Bigger God

Go out and stand before me on the mountain," the Lord told him. And as Elijah stood there, the Lord passed by, and a mighty windstorm hit the mountain. It was such a terrible blast that the rocks were torn loose, but the Lord was not in the wind. After the wind there was an earthquake, but the Lord was not in the earthquake."

**–1 KINGS 19:11 NLT**

God is the Alpha and the Omega, the beginning and the end. Trusting in the big and small is how I finally had the courage to write this second devotional journal. Let's ponder for a moment, if you honestly exercised full trust in the Lord, what might your life look like? What radical things might God call you to? If you had enough faith, what might you do that would require full dependence on God? Would you quit your job and enter full time ministry? Would you open up your home and host a life group? Would you go back to college or get your GED? What would you do differently if you knew you wouldn't fail? The promises of God often lose their power in our lives because God himself has become small in our eyes. We may be able to recite God's promises by the dozens but in our hearts, God is no longer the king who conquered armies and divided a valley to make dry land on the bottom of the sea floor. He is no longer the shepherd who seeks his sheep and keeps them safe behind his staff. He is no longer the Lord who walks on waves and calls the dead back from the grave. Slowly, subtly, we have forgotten God's power, God's wisdom and God's tenderness.

When the promises of God seem powerless to quiet our fears, soothe our grief, lift our worries, or motivate our obedience, we need to do more than simply hear His promises again. We need to behold the God who gives them. As I was reading this leadership book, I came across this quote from Oswald Chambers, "The great hindrance in spiritual life is that we will look for big things to do. 'Jesus took a towel and began to wash the disciples' feet.'" That was enough to bring tears to my eyes, God had my attention. I had assumed an attitude of thinking my "big works" would please God more than any small scale act I could do. Yes, Jesus did many awesome signs and wonders while on earth and we love to read about them and point them out to others. We quickly forget all the seemingly little ways Jesus was fully obedient to His Father God. Along with washing the disciples' feet, He had compassion on the needy, spoke encouragement, told stories to demonstrate God's goodness, taught and prayed for His friends, played with children, suffered, went to church (temple), endured insults, forgave His enemies, and ate with friends. All Jesus did was for the glory of God. He is our perfect example in becoming small to allow God to be big. Even our small acts of obedience, done out of trust in our Lord, are filled with the full power of God's grace. A heart set on living in servitude is what God desires; obedience is obedience. God's big yet simple and small approach is shown in the interaction between him and Elijah in 1 Kings 19:11-13, scripture reads "And behold, the Lord passed by, and a great and strong wind tore the mountains and broke in pieces the rocks before the Lord, but the Lord was not in the wind. And after the wind an earthquake, but the Lord was not in the earthquake. And after the earthquake a fire, but the Lord was not in the fire. And after the fire the sound of a low whisper. And when Elijah heard it, he wrapped his face in his cloak and went out and stood at the entrance of the cave. And behold, there came a voice to him..." God is big but He will meet you where you are even in the small places. So know this, God is in the subtle and low whispers, so make sure your frequency is turned up so you can hear Him.

. . . . . . . . . . . . . . . . . . . . . . . . . . . . . . . . . . . . . . . . . . . . . . . . . . . . . . . . .

. . . . . . . . . . . . . . . . . . . . . . . . . . . . . . . . . . . . . . . . . . . . . . . . . . . . . . . . .

. . . . . . . . . . . . . . . . . . . . . . . . . . . . . . . . . . . . . . . . . . . . . . . . . . . . . . . . .

. . . . . . . . . . . . . . . . . . . . . . . . . . . . . . . . . . . . . . . . . . . . . . . . . . . . . . . . .

. . . . . . . . . . . . . . . . . . . . . . . . . . . . . . . . . . . . . . . . . . . . . . . . . . . . . . . . .

. . . . . . . . . . . . . . . . . . . . . . . . . . . . . . . . . . . . . . . . . . . . . . . . . . . . . . . . .

. . . . . . . . . . . . . . . . . . . . . . . . . . . . . . . . . . . . . . . . . . . . . . . . . . . . . . . . .

## Prayer for Today

Lord, forgive me for making the all too common error of thinking You are more pleased with the world-changing evangelist than the community changing, obedient woman who shares Christ with others. You are still God in the biggest challenges or the smallest decisions we make. Thank you for being God. Amen

# Taming the Tongue

*Wise words satisfy like a good meal; the right words bring satisfaction.*
**– PROVERBS 18:20 NLT**

Our words can be a blessing or a weapon. In any human relationship we're in, we must take into consideration the potency and power of our words. Isn't that why communication is so tricky? We can beat around the bush or be blunt with our words. We can send daggers with insults or refresh a soul with compliments. We can gossip about a coworker and then greet them with a smile in the blink of an eye. James explains this dilemma well in James 3:10 when he writes, "From the same mouth come blessing and cursing." This hits home for a lot of us because there have been times when we have said some encouraging words to others and moments later with the same tongue we nearly cuss someone out for cutting us off on the freeway in rush hour traffic. Taming the tongue is something that takes discipline and divine intervention by the Holy Spirit. It must be intentional and deliberate. No matter whether you're a parent, a pastor or a player on the football team, we all have to be responsible with our words and watch the things we say as well as how we say them. As believers and followers of Christ, it is our duty and call to be a reflection of God's light in dark places and the first way we can be a witness to others is by our words followed by our actions in love. Our words have the power to make or break someone. Why not use them for building others up and bringing glory to our Heavenly Father?

. . . . . . . . . . . . . . . . . . . . . . . . . . . . . . . . . . . . . . . . . . . . . . . . . . . . . . . . . .

. . . . . . . . . . . . . . . . . . . . . . . . . . . . . . . . . . . . . . . . . . . . . . . . . . . . . . . . . .

. . . . . . . . . . . . . . . . . . . . . . . . . . . . . . . . . . . . . . . . . . . . . . . . . . . . . . . . . .

. . . . . . . . . . . . . . . . . . . . . . . . . . . . . . . . . . . . . . . . . . . . . . . . . . . . . . . . . .

. . . . . . . . . . . . . . . . . . . . . . . . . . . . . . . . . . . . . . . . . . . . . . . . . . . . . . . . . .

. . . . . . . . . . . . . . . . . . . . . . . . . . . . . . . . . . . . . . . . . . . . . . . . . . . . . . . . . .

. . . . . . . . . . . . . . . . . . . . . . . . . . . . . . . . . . . . . . . . . . . . . . . . . . . . . . . . . .

## Prayer for Today

Father God I cringe when I recall the negative words I have uttered that have brought pain to others. I thank You that You have the power to wipe the guilt away with Your blood which forgives and cleanses me from all unrighteousness. I don't have to walk around condemned any longer. I am forgiven. I am cleansed. Help me master my mouth and encourage others with my words. In Jesus Name, Amen!

# Boomerangs

You must serve only the Lord your God. If you do, I will bless you with food and water, and I will protect you from illness.

**– EXODUS 23:25 NLT**

There comes a time when you realize that this battle is not yours, it's the Lord's. Over the years, my husband and I have mentored various married couples on how to set realistic smart goals for their marriage. Marriages are one of the most difficult relationships to maintain, sustain and even retain if you don't have God intertwined and woven in the tapestry of your relationship. Being in tandem with other people who have their own ideologies, past pain and hurtful experiences can be a challenge because it's natural and expected that you will not see eye to eye all of the time. Battles can be blessings in disguise. Every battle has a hidden lesson for either growth, opportunity, perspective and truth. When you try to fight battles in your own ability you will miss the opportunity of leveraging a solid fool proof, God-strategic plan. The idea of fear boomerangs until you catch it, kill it and move on. God sometimes creates the atmosphere for battles and struggles either to allow it to test your faith. But remember Beloved, it may look like your marriage is surrounded by chaos but know that if you're a believer, all you need to do is call on Jesus and you will be surrounded by a host of angels and His presence. If you don't have the strength, you'll have to learn to rely on Christ's strength, which is always enough. And even if you're in a place where you feel like you're all out of love, you can rely on His love that never runs out. When you are faithful, God will be faithful to you. When you bless others, you will be blessed. Be ready for your next boomerang blessing, because when you do it in the name of God and to give him glory, trust and believe that you will be getting a boomerang blessing in return.

*Day*

**20**

. . . . . . . . . . . . . . . . . . . . . . . . . . . . . . . . . . . . . . . . . . . . . . . . . .

. . . . . . . . . . . . . . . . . . . . . . . . . . . . . . . . . . . . . . . . . . . . . . . . . .

. . . . . . . . . . . . . . . . . . . . . . . . . . . . . . . . . . . . . . . . . . . . . . . . . .

. . . . . . . . . . . . . . . . . . . . . . . . . . . . . . . . . . . . . . . . . . . . . . . . . .

. . . . . . . . . . . . . . . . . . . . . . . . . . . . . . . . . . . . . . . . . . . . . . . . . .

. . . . . . . . . . . . . . . . . . . . . . . . . . . . . . . . . . . . . . . . . . . . . . . . . .

. . . . . . . . . . . . . . . . . . . . . . . . . . . . . . . . . . . . . . . . . . . . . . . . . .

## Prayer for Today

Dear Lord, you are so generous. Thank You for the abundance of Your grace, mercy, love, and truth. Help me to live generously and to give open-handedly just as You do with me. In Jesus' name, Amen.

# Fly Little One

For the Lord is the Spirit, and wherever the Spirit of the Lord is, there is freedom.
**– 2 CORINTHIANS 3:17 NLT**

Birds fly in flocks, but eagles soar. Eagles are free and confident to fly alone. They don't follow the flock. They have the keenest eyesight of all birds. They fly high. The higher the eagle flies, the sharper its vision becomes. They can see over a two mile radius. Eagles set their eyes on their prey and do not lose sight of it. Its focus is set and it goes after the prey. Like the eagle, we need to come up higher. You cannot go higher unless you go deeper. You must be strong in order to fly high. A fully grown eagle is not afraid of a storm because it flies above it. We all have those days where we let the negative thoughts that we're not good enough, not pretty enough or not smart enough invade our minds. It's easy to lose hope in these situations and to feel like it would be easier to just give up. However, today is the day you recognize that the cage door has always been wide open waiting for you to take flight. You've been equipped and ready for quite some time so there is no reason to fly back into your cage of comfort. You were created for more.

Oftentimes when God has equipped us for flight we fall back into fear. Trust me on this, no one is more aware of your limitations than you. The Bible clearly says that "those who put their trust in the Lord will renew their strength and soar on wings like eagles." Isaiah 40:31 When we put our trust in the Lord we are not working in our ability but in the ability of God. The same passage in Isaiah also says "when they run they will not grow weary, they will walk and they will not faint." The strength that comes from the Lord will keep us going and fill us with peace, vacating anxiety and giving confidence. You know your insecurities, weaknesses, and flaws better than anyone else. You even know your hidden thoughts and motivations. Because you know yourself so well. When God calls us up, we so often answer Him with, "but God…" Our "buts" often weigh us down, keeping us from pushing forward. Freedom in Christ doesn't come with a return address. When He sets you free, you're free. Your comfort zone might not kill you, but it will keep you from the purposes of God.

It's time to take flight. God's got you!

# 21

. . . . . . . . . . . . . . . . . . . . . . . . . . . . . . . . . . . . . . . . . . . . . . .

. . . . . . . . . . . . . . . . . . . . . . . . . . . . . . . . . . . . . . . . . . . . . . .

. . . . . . . . . . . . . . . . . . . . . . . . . . . . . . . . . . . . . . . . . . . . . . .

. . . . . . . . . . . . . . . . . . . . . . . . . . . . . . . . . . . . . . . . . . . . . . .

. . . . . . . . . . . . . . . . . . . . . . . . . . . . . . . . . . . . . . . . . . . . . . .

. . . . . . . . . . . . . . . . . . . . . . . . . . . . . . . . . . . . . . . . . . . . . . .

. . . . . . . . . . . . . . . . . . . . . . . . . . . . . . . . . . . . . . . . . . . . . . .

## Prayer for Today

God, in Your word you reassure me that if I put my trust in You, I can run and not grow weary, I will walk and not faint. I will mount up on wings as an eagle and soar to a higher destiny in You. Give me the wisdom and understanding to use my fears as fuel to walk in my purpose. In Jesus Name, Amen.

# Good Morning God

How wonderful are the good things
you keep for those who honor you!
Everyone knows how good you are,
how securely you protect those who trust you.
**— PSALM 31:19 GNT**

Have you ever considered how good the Lord is to you? Can I admit something that I do sometimes frequently at work? I often jump into a conversation at the beginning of the day and I don't even start off by saying good morning. I am finally realizing this and now I catch myself because honestly that is rude and inconsiderate. You never know what the person you're interacting with is dealing with so instead you should at least pause and give him or her a positive greeting or salutation. I think it's the same consideration you should give God when you are blessed to see another day, by starting the morning with a good morning and thank you God for giving me another day to make an impact and live out my God-given purpose. Imagine how your day would change if you began it by saturating yourself with God's Word.

Every day you're alive is a gift from God and it's a day full of promise and great potential because our Creator has given it to us. Think for a moment if you're at work right now. You have a job. Didn't God provide that for you? There are many people who aren't employed. It applies as you go grocery shopping or walk through department stores buying what you need. You may have a car to drive, a house to live in and a bed to sleep in. All of these and more should make us grateful. Yes, there are days when we don't feel like being grateful for His goodness. Nothing goes right and the day is not full of promise or joy. We wish we'd never got out of bed. We say, let the world go on without me. However, in spite of that, we need to remember that every day, regardless of what happens, is a brand new gift and should be opened with loving care. The day will continue as other days do, even if you're not happy about it. Time doesn't stop because you do. It continues on.

. . . . . . . . . . . . . . . . . . . . . . . . . . . . . . . . . . . . . . . . . . . . . . . . . . . . . . .

. . . . . . . . . . . . . . . . . . . . . . . . . . . . . . . . . . . . . . . . . . . . . . . . . . . . . . .

. . . . . . . . . . . . . . . . . . . . . . . . . . . . . . . . . . . . . . . . . . . . . . . . . . . . . . .

. . . . . . . . . . . . . . . . . . . . . . . . . . . . . . . . . . . . . . . . . . . . . . . . . . . . . . .

. . . . . . . . . . . . . . . . . . . . . . . . . . . . . . . . . . . . . . . . . . . . . . . . . . . . . . .

. . . . . . . . . . . . . . . . . . . . . . . . . . . . . . . . . . . . . . . . . . . . . . . . . . . . . . .

. . . . . . . . . . . . . . . . . . . . . . . . . . . . . . . . . . . . . . . . . . . . . . . . . . . . . . .

### Prayer for Today

Good morning, Lord! Today's a new day, a chance for a new start. Yesterday is gone and with it any regrets, mistakes, or failures I may have experienced. It's a good day to be glad and give thanks, and I do, Lord. Thank You for today, a new opportunity to love, give, and be all that You want me to be. In Jesus Name, Amen.

# Do it Afraid

...but even in darkness I cannot hide from you. To you the night shines as bright as day. Darkness and light are the same to you.

**– PSALM 139:12 NLT**

I have been afraid of scary movies for as long as I can remember. I hate that feeling when the movie is over and my mind is racing and it's time to walk downstairs in the dark to my bedroom from the media room. I have had many days where my life felt a lot like a horror movie due to some of the tough things I experienced in my life that have left me feeling vulnerable and alone. I felt that familiar weakness in my knees I get when I don't know what my next step will be or if I am even stepping in the right direction. Fear felt like it would suffocate me as I considered whether to keep walking or resume the fetal position. It was in one of those dark hours that God spoke these words to me through the Psalms, "even the darkness is not dark to Me...darkness and light are alike to Me." I find comfort knowing that God is not waiting for me on the other side of darkness and that my darkness is not darkness to Him at all. I cling to this truth knowing that God is the same in the darkness as He is in the light.

Maybe it's not a horror movie for you. Maybe it is a top fear for most and that is the fear of failure. Have you ever been so afraid of failing at something that you decided not to try it at all? Or has a fear of failure meant that you undermined your own efforts to avoid the possibility of a bigger failure? I believe most of us have probably experienced this at one time or another. The fear of failing can be immobilizing. It can cause us to do nothing, and therefore resist moving forward. But when we allow fear to stop our forward progress in life, we're likely to miss out on some great opportunities along the way. And that is a shame. The possibility of failure is not something we enjoy. We all fall short of what we ought to do. We fail in our marriages, in raising our children, in our friendships, in school, in our careers and often with devastating consequences. It's no wonder, then, that at one time or another we all have a fear of failure. Fear is the devil's favorite tool in the toolbox of schemes he uses to destroy God's plan for you. He uses it to hold you back and prevent progress in your relationships and more. I have heard that when fear knocks on our door, we should send faith to answer. We can conquer fear, but only with faith. When the devil tells us, "You can't," we should remember God tells us, "You can." Even though we may feel fear, we can move forward in faith. God never stops loving us and doesn't even become angry with us because we choose fear, but it does make Him sad because He wants us to live the best life we can live. He sent Jesus so we could have life and have it abundantly. Remember, courage isn't the absence of fear; it is learning how to move forward in the presence of fear. Courageous people do what they believe in their hearts they should do, no matter how they feel or what doubts fill their minds. When you take ownership of your problems and open your heart to God, He will help bring light into darkness so that you can be free.

· · · · · · · · · · · · · · · · · · · · · · · · · · · · · · · · · · · · · · · · · · · · · · · ·

· · · · · · · · · · · · · · · · · · · · · · · · · · · · · · · · · · · · · · · · · · · · · · · ·

· · · · · · · · · · · · · · · · · · · · · · · · · · · · · · · · · · · · · · · · · · · · · · · ·

· · · · · · · · · · · · · · · · · · · · · · · · · · · · · · · · · · · · · · · · · · · · · · · ·

· · · · · · · · · · · · · · · · · · · · · · · · · · · · · · · · · · · · · · · · · · · · · · · ·

· · · · · · · · · · · · · · · · · · · · · · · · · · · · · · · · · · · · · · · · · · · · · · · ·

· · · · · · · · · · · · · · · · · · · · · · · · · · · · · · · · · · · · · · · · · · · · · · · ·

## Prayer for Today

Dear God, our Lord, you have commanded us to be courageous and full of strength. You tell us to neither be terrified nor be discouraged, for wherever we go, You are with us. Help me to hold onto Your word and be calm in Your promise. Make my faith in You continue to grow so I cannot be shaken by any situation. I need courage, I need strength. I need You, God. Amen.

# DAY 24
## Hey You

Be completely humble and gentle; be patient, bearing with one another in love.
**—EPHESIANS 4:2 NIV**

Hey You, let's just set the record straight. Humility doesn't mean you lack confidence or courage; it simply means you're led by love instead of selfishness. If you keep telling the same sad small story, you will keep living the same sad small life. We all have little fears we have not addressed. These fears lie dormant until you are called upon by life to confront and overcome them. It doesn't really matter what you are afraid of. What matters is trusting yourself enough to confront it, walk through it and survive it. Just take this moment to pause....... When God breathed His life into you, He breathed perseverance, determination, strength, courage and endurance. That means you have staying power; you can outlast every attack. Life may throw you some curveballs but every setback is a setup for a greater comeback. If you will stay in faith and have a never-say-die attitude, God will turn every battle into a blessing! Praying humbly before you talk not only enlists God's help but it also moves you to listen more closely and be slower to speak.

. . . . . . . . . . . . . . . . . . . . . . . . . . . . . . . . . . . . . . . . . . . . . . . . . . .

. . . . . . . . . . . . . . . . . . . . . . . . . . . . . . . . . . . . . . . . . . . . . . . . . . .

. . . . . . . . . . . . . . . . . . . . . . . . . . . . . . . . . . . . . . . . . . . . . . . . . . .

. . . . . . . . . . . . . . . . . . . . . . . . . . . . . . . . . . . . . . . . . . . . . . . . . . .

. . . . . . . . . . . . . . . . . . . . . . . . . . . . . . . . . . . . . . . . . . . . . . . . . . .

. . . . . . . . . . . . . . . . . . . . . . . . . . . . . . . . . . . . . . . . . . . . . . . . . . .

. . . . . . . . . . . . . . . . . . . . . . . . . . . . . . . . . . . . . . . . . . . . . . . . . . .

## Prayer for Today

God, please enlighten my mind with truth, inflame my heart with love, inspire my will with courage and enrich my life with service. Pardon what I have been, sanctify what I am, and order what I shall be. In Jesus' name, Amen.

# Brave Ain't Easy

The wicked flee when no one pursues, but the righteous are bold as a lion.
**—PROVERBS 28:1 ESV**

Be Brave. Easy said but not easily done. Over the past several years, I've heard various people call me brave because they saw the outward acts of bravery such as relocating with my job to three different states, launching my own company and brand, starting a podcast and writing a book.

When I look over the course of my life, it is definitely the road-less-traveled that I have opted for. But I have a confession to make — every time I do something new, I feel scared. I mean seriously scared. It may even surprise you to know that every single time I make a personal post or do a podcast, I get nervous. And, the more intimate, real and raw the podcast or the more vulnerable and exposed I feel, the greater the fear and nervousness sets in. The greater the vulnerability, the greater the exposure. I feel as if every time I post something, it is putting a piece of myself out there, a part of myself which is open to criticism, rejection and it even exposes my own biases and blind-spots. This is really hard to come to terms with. I know it's necessary because it's what I want to be doing with my life and I know that it is the only way to learn and grow; but still it's not always easy. The Oxford dictionary defines brave as: Ready to face and endure danger or pain, showing courage. Bravery and courage are intertwined, maybe two sides of the same coin — and on the other side, lies fear. So, this means to know bravery, we need to know fear. Our minds fear everything that isn't known; our mind's (ego) job is to keep us safe and protected, in the known. Which, in a nutshell, means that anything new including the future is unknown and will produce a certain amount of fear. Just think about that for a minute.

So when you think about making brave and bold queen moves, it means to first acknowledge your fears. Dissect them, shine a light on them to see that (more often than not) they are not as scary as you imagined. Usually, when we shine a light on our fears, we discover them to have no more substance than a curtain blowing against a chair in the breeze. So, for me, my process in trying to be brave always comes down to acknowledging my fears. Then comes the necessary first courageous step, and no matter how many times you do it, it is still scary as hell. Wait, can I say hell in a Christian based book? Oh well, I just did! Anyways, bravery does NOT mean having no fear, it means feeling the fear and having the courage to do it anyway. And trust me when I say this, none of this comes easy to me but it takes some grit, gumption and action. Like a muscle, the more you flex it, the stronger it gets. Stop using it, and it weakens. I can tell you that the moments of my greatest fears, those times when I was sure I was going to wimp out under the pressure of it all, have also been the open doors to the greatest changes in my life. So I step out, full of fear, but trusting that God is on the other side in new and wonderful ways. And so far, He always is. He will be for you too. So today, choose bravery, and tell five people (a relative, a friend, a coworker, a mentor, and a neighbor) that you have begun this 100-day journey toward a braver life and encourage them to join you in this quest towards bravery.

Day

25

· · · · · · · · · · · · · · · · · · · · · · · · · · · · · · · · · · · · · · · · · · · · · · · · ·

· · · · · · · · · · · · · · · · · · · · · · · · · · · · · · · · · · · · · · · · · · · · · · · · ·

· · · · · · · · · · · · · · · · · · · · · · · · · · · · · · · · · · · · · · · · · · · · · · · · ·

· · · · · · · · · · · · · · · · · · · · · · · · · · · · · · · · · · · · · · · · · · · · · · · · ·

· · · · · · · · · · · · · · · · · · · · · · · · · · · · · · · · · · · · · · · · · · · · · · · · ·

· · · · · · · · · · · · · · · · · · · · · · · · · · · · · · · · · · · · · · · · · · · · · · · · ·

· · · · · · · · · · · · · · · · · · · · · · · · · · · · · · · · · · · · · · · · · · · · · · · · ·

## Prayer for Today

Dear Lord, As I go through my days facing each of the situations before me, I pray that You give me the strength to be patient as I wait for You to move in every single one. Help me to be brave and courageous when the fear grows strong and the time passes so slowly. Help me to cast fear far away as I keep my eyes on You in every single situation today. Amen

# Warrior Princess

Don't be afraid," the prophet answered. "Those who are with us are more than those who are with them.

**– 2 KINGS 6:16 NIV**

Have you ever met a real warrior? I'm not talking about Hollywood's ridiculous version of the warrior from a reality show. I'm talking about a true warrior. They're a different breed. Warriors carry themselves differently than most people. They move and speak with purpose. They are not people who usually stand out in the crowd. However, others will look to them in times of great difficulty. You won't hear a true warrior bragging about how awesome they are or about the things they have done. A warrior may have a sense of humor, but they never play the fool. Warriors usually have a quiet confidence that comes from another source. When you meet a true warrior, you will know it. Simply put, warriors operate differently than most people. One of the things that seperates warriors from others is the price they are willing to pay. Warriors train for long hours. They endure great difficulties and pain. They are willing to sacrifice their own personal comfort, preferences, and selfish desires. Every sacrifice is made in the service of a greater cause. Few people become warriors because they are unwilling to pay the real price. Most people are unwilling to make significant and long-term sacrifices. The price is high to be a true warrior. Plus, the costs are ongoing. Sacrifice goes well beyond some initial period of training. Warriors make sacrifice a lifestyle. Your private relationship with God will produce public manifestation.

Warriors pray before they make decisions. Warriors pray before they go to work. Warriors pray before they go to school. Warriors pray before they enter the boardroom. Warriors pray before the job interview. Warriors pray for their marriage, their children and their legacy. The strategy of warfare you have learned will give you supernatural wisdom in governing your family affairs, rule your emotions, fortify your marriage, shift kingdoms, silence the enemy and rescue the people God has placed in your pathway. You are a warrior. God has equipped you to lead a warrior's life. You do not have to cower in fear or be anxious for the future. God is your King, your Commanding Officer and can show up to the battle lines ready for war. There is no need for you to shrink back. No need to apologize. It's time for war. Are you ready?

. . . . . . . . . . . . . . . . . . . . . . . . . . . . . . . . . . . . . . . . . . . . . . . . . . . . . . . .

. . . . . . . . . . . . . . . . . . . . . . . . . . . . . . . . . . . . . . . . . . . . . . . . . . . . . . . .

. . . . . . . . . . . . . . . . . . . . . . . . . . . . . . . . . . . . . . . . . . . . . . . . . . . . . . . .

. . . . . . . . . . . . . . . . . . . . . . . . . . . . . . . . . . . . . . . . . . . . . . . . . . . . . . . .

. . . . . . . . . . . . . . . . . . . . . . . . . . . . . . . . . . . . . . . . . . . . . . . . . . . . . . . .

. . . . . . . . . . . . . . . . . . . . . . . . . . . . . . . . . . . . . . . . . . . . . . . . . . . . . . . .

## Prayer for Today

God, today I claim victory over the enemy by putting on the whole armor of God! I put on the girdle of truth. May I stand firm in the truth of Your word so I will not be a victim of satan's lies. I put on the breastplate of righteousness! May it guard my heart from evil so I will remain pure and holy, protected by the blood of Jesus Christ. I put on the shoes of peace! May I stand firm in the good news of the gospel so Your peace will shine through me and be a light to everyone I encounter. I take the shield of faith! May I be ready for satan's fiery darts of doubt, denial, and deceit so I will not be vulnerable to spiritual defeat. I put on the helmet of salvation! May I keep my mind focused on You so satan will not have a stronghold on my thoughts. I take the sword of the spirit which is Your holy word! May the two-edged sword of Your Word be ready in my hands so I can expose the tempting words of satan. By faith your warrior has put on the whole armor of God! I am prepared to live this day in spiritual victory! In Jesus Name, Amen.

# Thank Ya, You Did it Again

Give freely and become more wealthy; be stingy and lose everything.
The generous will prosper; those who refresh others will themselves be refreshed.

**– PROVERBS 11:24-25 NLT**

Go ahead, count your blessings and give thanks this week. Really do that. Be sure that you are praising God, knowing that "every perfect gift is from above" James 1:17. He deserves all the credit. If you don't understand that, you won't understand the purpose of life. Displaying gratitude is a great practice. But let's be honest, it's really easy to do and all too often it can keep us focused on ourselves and what we have. We may nod our heads at God but then go right on shoveling mashed potatoes into our faces. How about getting more serious this year? Don't stop at being thankful for what you have. Take inventory of your blessings and then give them away. Yes, that's right, give them away. Many of us women go through cycles of downsizing and "purging" of what we own. This is good, but why do we participate in this cycle at all? We give, but then we take stuff up again. If we were to look at how Christ dealt with possessions we would see a different lifestyle. He depended fully on his Father to provide for Him as He traveled and went seeking and saving the lost. Jesus never worried about how His needs would be met but they were. Jesus didn't even have a place to call home during His ministry. "And Jesus said to him, "Foxes have holes, and birds of the air have nests, but the Son of Man has nowhere to lay his head." Luke 9:58. He was constantly surrounded by crowds whom He ministered to, often sharing what He had available like fish and bread (Matt. 14:13-21). Jesus also walked the grain fields with His disciples where they found lunch "and His disciples were hungry, and they began to pluck heads of grain and to eat." Matt. 12:1. This was only done by those who did not have enough food of their own to eat. By the time Jesus died on the cross His only possessions were the clothes on his back and even those were divided up and taken away. We need to do a better job at looking like Jesus in this area.

We may not sell our homes and walk the fields for dinner, but come on, we aren't even in the ballpark of Christ-likeness here. So time to go beyond the "thanks" and get serious about the "giving." You may find yourself parting with material possessions like jewelry, clothing, collections, hobby items, a vehicle or even careers. What you do keep, you need to share and use for the glory of God. Your home should be a ministry outpost, where people gather to be fed from your pantry and the Word of God. You could become foster parents, host Bible studies or house those in need. Or, God may call you to look very much like Jesus and sell everything and trust Him in mission work. Finally, I encourage you to give up the blessings that usually top every list: family and friends. You need to give them to God. Entrust them to His care at all times. You do this by praying for them daily, sharing God's Word and by understanding that He has full authority over their lives. Lovingly push all those who are precious to you toward Jesus.

. . . . . . . . . . . . . . . . . . . . . . . . . . . . . . . . . . . . . . . . . . . . . . . . . . . . . . . .

. . . . . . . . . . . . . . . . . . . . . . . . . . . . . . . . . . . . . . . . . . . . . . . . . . . . . . . .

. . . . . . . . . . . . . . . . . . . . . . . . . . . . . . . . . . . . . . . . . . . . . . . . . . . . . . . .

. . . . . . . . . . . . . . . . . . . . . . . . . . . . . . . . . . . . . . . . . . . . . . . . . . . . . . . .

. . . . . . . . . . . . . . . . . . . . . . . . . . . . . . . . . . . . . . . . . . . . . . . . . . . . . . . .

. . . . . . . . . . . . . . . . . . . . . . . . . . . . . . . . . . . . . . . . . . . . . . . . . . . . . . . .

. . . . . . . . . . . . . . . . . . . . . . . . . . . . . . . . . . . . . . . . . . . . . . . . . . . . . . . .

### Prayer for Today

Heavenly Father, help us have the desire and ability to reflect the generous quality of You and give freely of all we have been blessed with. We praise You for all of the blessings throughout this week, month and even quarter of the year. Help us remain in the posture of gratitude to continue to worship You in every blessing. In Jesus' name, Amen.

# DAY 28
# *You Got Next*

So those who are last now will be first then, and those who are first will be last.
**– MATTHEW 20:16 NLT**

What if God were to tell you at this very moment or this week that you got next ? What would you do? Would you be ready? Would your house be in order? Would your financial analysis or business plan/ vision statement be ready to articulate and share? Would you already have a circle or core group of believers that were in your inner circle to keep you in prayer? I know that there were a lot of questions asked all at once, and I am not seeking answers because we all know that when God says go, He equips. And when He equips us, He pulls together what you have already begun and accelerates it. Many times, we have been praying for the "thing" or the next big thing to happen and when God answers and says "you're next," we respond by saying "Umm, how about you give me a raincheck God and check back with me in a few months." Now sometimes that works because you just hijack your blessing and mess up the timing. But many times, that does not work because you have to remember that when you say NO to God's GO, you're frankly out of order and out of line and disobedient. Ouch....I know you're probably saying Kara it's too early or too late for all of this! However, God is asking us to be ready to do the convenient, the inconvenient, the easy, the difficult, the challenging and the unusual for the kingdom of God. And when it comes to bringing more and sharing the good news of the gospel we need to push back those shoulders and say "alright, I'm ready if you're ready God." When God instructs, He guides and when He leads, you should follow. Delayed obedience is still disobedience. One of the most common reasons people fall short of the will of God in their lives is by not doing what He has told you to do.

Think about Simon and Andrew. When God told them what He had in store for them to become fishers of men. The word says immediately, they dropped their nets and joined Him. They didn't ask any questions. They didn't try to negotiate different terms and or even a different time period. They didn't say wait hold up, let me gather my stuff. They basically said already let's do this. Count us in. This reminds me of when we took the kids to Disneyworld and we got these Disney Fast Passes. They were like having a golden ticket at the park. The fast pass allows you to skip the line and move to the front of the line regardless of how long the line is. This is like when God says "you're next." He is basically telling you, you have been faithfully waiting in line, sowing your seeds, reading the word, remaining obedient and now you got next. You have been promoted, you have gained access, you now have been approved for the loan, the college application, the background check. You got next so go! God is calling you. He knows you are equipped, you are ready and you are in position for the new territories, new places and opportunities that are on the horizon. Go confidently and boldly.

. . . . . . . . . . . . . . . . . . . . . . . . . . . . . . . . . . . . . . . . . . . . . . . . . . . . . .

. . . . . . . . . . . . . . . . . . . . . . . . . . . . . . . . . . . . . . . . . . . . . . . . . . . . . .

. . . . . . . . . . . . . . . . . . . . . . . . . . . . . . . . . . . . . . . . . . . . . . . . . . . . . .

. . . . . . . . . . . . . . . . . . . . . . . . . . . . . . . . . . . . . . . . . . . . . . . . . . . . . .

. . . . . . . . . . . . . . . . . . . . . . . . . . . . . . . . . . . . . . . . . . . . . . . . . . . . . .

. . . . . . . . . . . . . . . . . . . . . . . . . . . . . . . . . . . . . . . . . . . . . . . . . . . . . .

. . . . . . . . . . . . . . . . . . . . . . . . . . . . . . . . . . . . . . . . . . . . . . . . . . . . . .

## *Prayer for Today*

Heavenly Father, I thank You for shaping and guiding my life and for this promotion. I am sure that it is You who has positioned me where I am now and for this reason, I am grateful. Lord, I pray that You help me to remain humble in my current promotion so that You may promote me again in due time, according to Your will and purpose. I pray that any promotions that are not from You will be undone. In Jesus' name, thank You, Lord. Amen.

# Check Your Roots

Therefore as you have received Christ Jesus the Lord, so walk in him, having been firmly rooted and now being built up in him and established in your faith, just as you were instructed, and overflowing with gratitude.

**– COLOSSIANS 2:6-7**

Over the past several days I have been doing some gardening and decided to dig up two of the large bushes in my flower bed. After a series of unexpected snow storms we experienced in Texas, I noticed this year that there were no blooms on the tree. I probably could have waited until later in the summer to see if they were going to bloom but I decided to uproot them. So I thought it was going to be an easy task until I started digging and digging. The first bush took two hours to uproot but the second one was easier. I realized that if I located the main hardy roots I can snip them and then apply some weight on the branches. The roots were deep but with a little labor I finally got them out. Just as a tree needs deep roots to withstand the storms and droughts, we also need to be deeply rooted in our faith. Although these bushes were hit by the winter mix earlier this year, their roots were solid and deeply rooted. Just think ladies, when we are well-watered, deep-rooted in our faith, we can also sustain those fall and winter seasons of our lives that sometimes bring uncertainty, doubt and insecurity. Allow me to take a quick detour and remind you that our unexpected is never unexpected to God. As you reflect during this season on your life, your struggles, your disappointments, your victories, your faith, and your hope, remember that God is God and we are not. Jesus' death on the cross was simultaneously foolishness to the wise in the world, to those who are perishing and a demonstration of the power and wisdom of God to those of us who believe. He doesn't always do things the way we might expect or wish He would. But when it comes to God, expect the unexpected. Faith in God certainly doesn't make us safe (as if we were living in a magical bubble in which nothing bad could happen and we were guaranteed success at every turn), but it does make us incredibly secure. Now that should make you shout on that! You are secure in Jesus Christ if you're a believer. Because He is faithful and good, we can trust and worship without always completely understanding. In this season, it is time to go back to your roots and reconnect with Christ. Start today and watch your spirit bloom.

· · · · · · · · · · · · · · · · · · · · · · · · · · · · · · · · · · · · · · · · · · ·

· · · · · · · · · · · · · · · · · · · · · · · · · · · · · · · · · · · · · · · · · · ·

· · · · · · · · · · · · · · · · · · · · · · · · · · · · · · · · · · · · · · · · · · ·

· · · · · · · · · · · · · · · · · · · · · · · · · · · · · · · · · · · · · · · · · · ·

· · · · · · · · · · · · · · · · · · · · · · · · · · · · · · · · · · · · · · · · · · ·

· · · · · · · · · · · · · · · · · · · · · · · · · · · · · · · · · · · · · · · · · · ·

· · · · · · · · · · · · · · · · · · · · · · · · · · · · · · · · · · · · · · · · · · ·

## Prayer for Today

Dear Lord, I pray that You plant me firmly in Your word and love. Sow my roots so deeply that I cannot be uprooted by the storms of life. Let me know that You are God and that You live in me. Help me love myself unconditionally so that I may be confident wherever I am. Teach me to love myself and to never doubt that I am Your beautiful daughter. In Jesus' name, Amen.

# Fiction or Fact

He says, "Be still, and know that I am God; I will be exalted among the nations, I will be exalted in the earth."

**– PSALM 46:10 NIV**

Think about the story you're living right now. Who wrote it? Did you consciously decide to create the reality you're currently living or was it mainly shaped by your parents, friends, spouse, school or the media? In 2021, I realized that I was living a story that I never fully wrote. It was a biography written by a guarded and fearful person rather than an autobiography written on faith and optimism. Many times we are living safe lives because it's easy and there is less resistance or opposition but that is fake and almost like you are in a fun house with multiple mirrors that are distorted and fragmented. Through a lot of prayer and seeking God, I learned that if I didn't like the story I was living, then it was time to change my perception. I know what you're thinking, yes that's hard especially if you have been living a fictitious life for a long time and you don't really know who the real you is anymore. If that's the case, start with envisioning how you'd write the next chapter of your story. Better yet, actually sit down and write it. Perception is merely a lens or mindset from which we view people, events and things. In other words, we believe what we perceive to be accurate and we create our own realities based on those perceptions. And although our perceptions seem very real, that doesn't mean they're necessarily factual. Today may be the day you need to adjust some of the dials on your life to get better reception or perception. Get rid of those rabbit ears and make the switch to digital. Your perception impacts your reception....Hmmm...think on that!

. . . . . . . . . . . . . . . . . . . . . . . . . . . . . . . . . . . . . . . . . . . . . . . . . . . . . . . . . . . . .

. . . . . . . . . . . . . . . . . . . . . . . . . . . . . . . . . . . . . . . . . . . . . . . . . . . . . . . . . . . . .

. . . . . . . . . . . . . . . . . . . . . . . . . . . . . . . . . . . . . . . . . . . . . . . . . . . . . . . . . . . . .

. . . . . . . . . . . . . . . . . . . . . . . . . . . . . . . . . . . . . . . . . . . . . . . . . . . . . . . . . . . . .

. . . . . . . . . . . . . . . . . . . . . . . . . . . . . . . . . . . . . . . . . . . . . . . . . . . . . . . . . . . . .

. . . . . . . . . . . . . . . . . . . . . . . . . . . . . . . . . . . . . . . . . . . . . . . . . . . . . . . . . . . . .

. . . . . . . . . . . . . . . . . . . . . . . . . . . . . . . . . . . . . . . . . . . . . . . . . . . . . . . . . . . . .

## Prayer for Today

O God, my strength, I believe that I can do all things through You who strengthens me. I ask that You have Your divine way in my life so that I can grow into this divine promotion that You have called me to. I pray that You will help me to be fearless as I enter new territories. Crush my fears. Help me act in power, love and with a sound mind. In Jesus' name, Amen.

# Embrace Your Awesomeness

And I am certain that God, who began the good work within you, will continue his work until it is finally finished on the day when Christ Jesus returns.

**– PHILIPPIANS 1:6 NLT**

We are a generation of women who have never worked harder to have it all, yet go to bed most nights worrying that we aren't enough. We're constantly asking "Why?" It doesn't matter if you're single, if you're married, if you're rich, poor, old, young, in college or a high school dropout. We're always looking around to see how we measure up against everyone around us and usually with all of this focusing on everyone else we fall short. The world is full of messages telling you that you're not good enough, smart enough, spiritual enough or even that you're too much. It's too easy to let those statements pull you down and suck the joy out of your day. However, I believe that our struggle with wondering if we're good enough goes back primarily to how much we trust God. We aren't struggling because of the specifics of our circumstances as much as we're struggling because of lack of trust in God to provide us what we need, to show us where we are supposed to go and even to guide us in what we should be doing in our life. Believe me, this day in the devotional is for me too. I mentor different age groups of women and I have found the universal theme between all of my mentees is that internal self-doubting voice. All of us have that internal voice that whispers lies and highlights the things we wish we could forget or hide. And you begin the unhealthy cycle of making personal statements that start off with "I should've....." This is the very statement that will lead you to unnecessary anxiety, stress, depression, obsessive behaviors and even other physical symptoms. Recently one of my mentees and I were discussing her goals of increasing her volunteerism and setting up a large program in the future, in which I told her it was great but what about now? I asked her what she could do on a small scale that aligned with her purpose that would still be a step towards her goal. She felt she needed to have completed staff work instantly, with the funding, vision statement, everything as she felt like she was inadequate. It is easy to lean on society's standards but those are the moments when you need to lean in on the word of God. Because He is the God of enough. No matter how you feel, speak over yourself, encourage yourself in the Lord. And remember, God says you are enough because HE is! You're enough because you were made in the image of God and carry His likeness in You.

. . . . . . . . . . . . . . . . . . . . . . . . . . . . . . . . . . . . . . . . . . . . . . . . . . . . . . . . . . . . .

. . . . . . . . . . . . . . . . . . . . . . . . . . . . . . . . . . . . . . . . . . . . . . . . . . . . . . . . . . . . .

. . . . . . . . . . . . . . . . . . . . . . . . . . . . . . . . . . . . . . . . . . . . . . . . . . . . . . . . . . . . .

. . . . . . . . . . . . . . . . . . . . . . . . . . . . . . . . . . . . . . . . . . . . . . . . . . . . . . . . . . . . .

. . . . . . . . . . . . . . . . . . . . . . . . . . . . . . . . . . . . . . . . . . . . . . . . . . . . . . . . . . . . .

. . . . . . . . . . . . . . . . . . . . . . . . . . . . . . . . . . . . . . . . . . . . . . . . . . . . . . . . . . . . .

. . . . . . . . . . . . . . . . . . . . . . . . . . . . . . . . . . . . . . . . . . . . . . . . . . . . . . . . . . . . .

## Prayer for Today

Almighty God, when my thoughts surge up and seek to shake my rest in You, when anxiety, agitation and fear rise up to disturb me, please remind me to bring everything in prayer to You, to lay it all at Your feet with thanksgiving for Your provision and care so that nothing will break the calm and security which I possess in You. I thank You merciful and gracious God that I can bring all my requests and burdens to You. In Jesus' name, Amen.

# DAY 32
## Level Up

"Forget the former things; do not dwell on the past. See, I am doing a new thing! Now it springs up; do you not perceive it? I am making a way in the desert and streams in the wasteland.
**– ISAIAH 43:18-20 NIV**

The thought of resigning from a job for almost 24 years gave me tremendous anxiety, panic, avoidance and doubt. These same feelings come up when ending any type of significant relationship. A break up is a break up whether it is with a person or a career. However, as the CEO of my company, I owed it to myself to make the best business moves for me.

Do you know that God's desire is for you to continuously make progress and advance to newer and higher levels in your life? He's always doing new things, charting new courses and opening new frontiers and He wants you to do the same. Every day when you wake up, you have two choices: continue to sleep with your dreams, or wake up and chase them. I want to challenge you today to get uncomfortable with your comfort zone and set out for new horizons. This means you shouldn't remain in one place for too long. There's always a greater and far more glorious level than where you are right now! There are no limits to how high you can go or how great you can become. This was the Apostle Paul's understanding that brought about the statement in Philippians 3:13-14, "I really do not think that I have already won it; the one thing I do, however, is to forget what is behind me and do my best to reach what is ahead. So I run straight toward the goal in order to win the prize, which is God's call through Christ Jesus to the life above." To act on this counsel, you must decide now to set new standards for your personality, academics, commitment in church, your giving, etc. You can also decide to take up the responsibility of reaching and changing the lives of more young people in your environment. Tell yourself, "It's time to move up higher!" and get to work on it. The real truth is that God uses everything in our life to conform us into His image. Today, I believe the Lord is saying to you, "Move up to your next and higher level in Me. Level up and set new standards for yourself in My Word!" Five, four, three, two, one....Level Up!

· · · · · · · · · · · · · · · · · · · · · · · · · · · · · · · · · · · · · · · · · · · · · · · · · ·

· · · · · · · · · · · · · · · · · · · · · · · · · · · · · · · · · · · · · · · · · · · · · · · · · ·

· · · · · · · · · · · · · · · · · · · · · · · · · · · · · · · · · · · · · · · · · · · · · · · · · ·

· · · · · · · · · · · · · · · · · · · · · · · · · · · · · · · · · · · · · · · · · · · · · · · · · ·

· · · · · · · · · · · · · · · · · · · · · · · · · · · · · · · · · · · · · · · · · · · · · · · · · ·

· · · · · · · · · · · · · · · · · · · · · · · · · · · · · · · · · · · · · · · · · · · · · · · · · ·

· · · · · · · · · · · · · · · · · · · · · · · · · · · · · · · · · · · · · · · · · · · · · · · · · ·

## Prayer for Today

Heavenly Father, I thank You because You made me with purpose. From my youth, You've shown me what to do in line with Your purpose for my life. I ask humbly that You will move my career from glory to glory, from one level of achievement to another this season as You advance and establish my career, business and outreach. I trust in Your word and believe it will come to pass. Thank You in advance for my testimony of advancement.

# DAY 33
## Confidently True

You will keep in perfect peace those whose minds are steadfast, because they trust in you.
**– ISAIAH 26:3 NIV**

We all have moments when we lack confidence. But God created you in His own image and He wants you to value yourself the way He sees you. Everyone experiences a lack of confidence from time to time. Have you ever had those days when nothing seems to go right? You spill your morning coffee. Your menstrual cycle came earlier than expected and you're wearing white pants. You get to work only to realize you left your work badge on the kitchen countertop. You're late for an important meeting. It feels like one thing after another and by the end of the day, you can't help but toss up your hands in defeat. It's days like those that leave us less confident and questioning our self-worth. It can be quite a complicated business. A lack of confidence can look very different on different people, depending on the circumstances. Some people lack confidence in their personal appearance. Others lack confidence in their ability to voice their opinions. Others lack confidence in their abilities. Renee Swope said, "Self-confidence has limited potential but God-confidence has unlimited possibility!" Of course, no-one is totally confident all the time. And it's very normal to feel less than stellar every once in a while. However, I encourage you to fully trust God. There is something so sweet when you experience the peace of God that gives you the confidence you need to get through. God never fails. There is nothing too hard for God! God can do more for you in one second than you can do in a lifetime. Trust in Him. Get in His presence and seek Him today.

*Day*

# 33

. . . . . . . . . . . . . . . . . . . . . . . . . . . . . . . . . . . . . . . . . . . . . . . . . . .

. . . . . . . . . . . . . . . . . . . . . . . . . . . . . . . . . . . . . . . . . . . . . . . . . . .

. . . . . . . . . . . . . . . . . . . . . . . . . . . . . . . . . . . . . . . . . . . . . . . . . . .

. . . . . . . . . . . . . . . . . . . . . . . . . . . . . . . . . . . . . . . . . . . . . . . . . . .

. . . . . . . . . . . . . . . . . . . . . . . . . . . . . . . . . . . . . . . . . . . . . . . . . . .

. . . . . . . . . . . . . . . . . . . . . . . . . . . . . . . . . . . . . . . . . . . . . . . . . . .

. . . . . . . . . . . . . . . . . . . . . . . . . . . . . . . . . . . . . . . . . . . . . . . . . . .

## *Prayer for Today*

Dear Heavenly Father, Your grace amazes me. I pray that I never get over the wonder of it. Thank You that even as I grow my whole life long, I can never outgrow Your grace. I pray that You transform me into Your image with ever-increasing glory until the day when my growth is complete and I finally see You face-to-face. It's in the name of my Savior, Jesus Christ that I pray, Amen.

# DAY 34
## Lean On God

Then Jesus said, "Did I not tell you that if you believe, you will see the glory of God?"
**– JOHN 11:40 NIV**

*"Sometimes in our lives we all have pain, we all have sorrow; but, if we are wise, We know that there's always tomorrow."* These are words from *"Lean On Me,"* the hit song written by Bill Withers in 1972. We are always told to have faith and to trust God. We need to lean on God when life is overwhelming because He is our strength, our lifeline and the one who directs our steps. We need to lean on Him when we don't have the answers, when the mountain we need to be moved doesn't move, when the flood water's rise and there is no way out. We desperately need Him. We need His presence, His peace, We need Him to be our refuge and our shield when life is hard to get us through those days we just want to give up. In certain situations, that is easier said than done. We sometimes think things will be easier if we take it into our own hands. Nobody ever said having faith would be easy, but it will be worth it and here is why. When God is your audience, you no longer need the opinions of people to sustain you. God knows everything we are going through at this very moment and everything we will go through in the future. He knows the best way to handle every situation so we get the best possible outcome and we need to trust Him with that. We need to follow His path and trust that He knows best, because He does. He knows the desires of your heart. If you trust in Him with the things that you want most, He will take care of it. He knows what is best for your life. If you feel like your goals are hard to achieve or even impossible, think again. Anything is possible with God. He has your back and will help you through anything, all you have to do is have faith. God knows exactly what He wants for your life. He has a purpose for you and has everything planned out. He knows who you are going to marry, how many kids you are going to have, what job you will have and every other detail of your life, both big and small. He knows what you are going to do tomorrow, next month and the years down the road. Do not doubt His plan, because He knows all and He has the perfect plan. Don't lose sight of who your God is! The beginning and the end, the one who spoke and at the mere sound of His voice galaxies and planets and stars and entire solar systems formed. The one who formed every animal, every plant and told every wave where they had to end. The one who set the earth on the exact tilt and sent it spinning around the sun. My God is not a purring kitten but a roaring lion, who loves you so much that He sent His one and only son to save you, right where you are in the middle of your situation. So get out of your own understanding and lean into the word of God today.

. . . . . . . . . . . . . . . . . . . . . . . . . . . . . . . . . . . . . . . . . . . . . . . . . . . . . . . . . . .

. . . . . . . . . . . . . . . . . . . . . . . . . . . . . . . . . . . . . . . . . . . . . . . . . . . . . . . . . . .

. . . . . . . . . . . . . . . . . . . . . . . . . . . . . . . . . . . . . . . . . . . . . . . . . . . . . . . . . . .

. . . . . . . . . . . . . . . . . . . . . . . . . . . . . . . . . . . . . . . . . . . . . . . . . . . . . . . . . . .

. . . . . . . . . . . . . . . . . . . . . . . . . . . . . . . . . . . . . . . . . . . . . . . . . . . . . . . . . . .

. . . . . . . . . . . . . . . . . . . . . . . . . . . . . . . . . . . . . . . . . . . . . . . . . . . . . . . . . . .

. . . . . . . . . . . . . . . . . . . . . . . . . . . . . . . . . . . . . . . . . . . . . . . . . . . . . . . . . . .

### Prayer for Today

Father, You welcome me into your presence—and that's a wonder in itself. More than I can imagine. Then You invite me to lean against You—and a bolt of self-reliance in me resists. But I want to trust You. To relax the weight of my fears and anxieties against You. To rest, to know how fully trustworthy You are. Help me, Father. In Jesus' name, Amen.

# DAY 35
## Grow in Grace

The grace of the Lord Jesus be with God's people. Amen.
**– REVELATIONS 22:21 NIV**

Every day, every moment, with every action you're planting something. There is a cumulative effect of your down seeds. Everything in life starts as a seed: a relationship, a marriage, a business, a church, etc. And nothing happens until the seed is planted. Whatever we see manifested in the world and in our life today began as a seed. And, every seed that is planted must be received by faith. When we sow a seed, we put it in God's hands then watch God graciously and mercifully send the miracle that we need based on our faith. No matter how small our faith seems to be, God will meet the needs and solve problems that appear as impossible mountains in our lives.

In John 12:24 Jesus said, "Unless a kernel of wheat falls to the ground and dies, it remains only a single seed. But if it dies, it produces many seeds."

Here's the principle of sowing and reaping: Whenever you have a need, you plant a seed. Whatever it is you need — more time, more energy, more money, more support, more relationships, more wisdom — just plant a seed. If you need more time, give more time to your kids. If you need more wisdom, share what wisdom you have with others. Give yourself away! It may not make sense to you to give away something that you need more of, but that is exactly the kind of attitude that God wants to bless and that will produce fruit in your life. When you have a need, don't gripe about it, don't wish about it, and you don't even have to pray about it — just plant a seed!

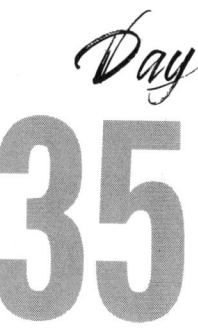

Day

35

. . . . . . . . . . . . . . . . . . . . . . . . . . . . . . . . . . . . . . . . . . . . . . . . . . . . .

. . . . . . . . . . . . . . . . . . . . . . . . . . . . . . . . . . . . . . . . . . . . . . . . . . . . .

. . . . . . . . . . . . . . . . . . . . . . . . . . . . . . . . . . . . . . . . . . . . . . . . . . . . .

. . . . . . . . . . . . . . . . . . . . . . . . . . . . . . . . . . . . . . . . . . . . . . . . . . . . .

. . . . . . . . . . . . . . . . . . . . . . . . . . . . . . . . . . . . . . . . . . . . . . . . . . . . .

. . . . . . . . . . . . . . . . . . . . . . . . . . . . . . . . . . . . . . . . . . . . . . . . . . . . .

. . . . . . . . . . . . . . . . . . . . . . . . . . . . . . . . . . . . . . . . . . . . . . . . . . . . .

## Prayer for Today

Dear Heavenly Father, Thank You for the principle of seed, time and harvest. Thank You that you give seed to the sower and bread to the eater. Teach me how to sow in righteousness and be a blessing to others and in return I know You will continue to bless me. In the name of Jesus Christ I pray. Amen.

# DAY 36
## You're Exceptional

But you are not like that, for you are a chosen people. You are royal priests, a holy nation, God's very own possession. As a result, you can show others the goodness of God, for he called you out of the darkness into his wonderful light.

**—1 PETER 2:9 NLT**

Beloved, did you know that you're exceptional? When God created you He did not make any mistakes! When something is exceptional it means that it stands out from the crowd. God does not want us to doubt our worth and abilities in Him. Did you know it's impossible to live at the brink of your greatness if you do not take time to discover it. You have God-given abilities and qualities to allow you to have successful relationships, excel in your career, dominate in school and have a strong family. There are people who think there's nothing special or unique about them. They believe they're ordinary and are comfortable to be referred to as such. You'll hear them say things like, "I am just doing my job, there's nothing special about what I do." Being exceptional means that you're uniquely different in some way, and that your beliefs and ideas can be inspiring to others or cause others to move and react positively. Understand that as a Christian, you're extra special; because you belong to the greatest family—the family of God—and to a special lineage of grace. This truth about who you are should inspire you to show God's love everywhere you go. Tell others about Him, so they too can join this glorious family and become citizens of God's Kingdom. Believe me when I say this, you have the right gifts, the right talents and the right personality. You're exceptional, so think and live accordingly.

. . . . . . . . . . . . . . . . . . . . . . . . . . . . . . . . . . . . . . . . . . . . . . . . . . . . . . . .

. . . . . . . . . . . . . . . . . . . . . . . . . . . . . . . . . . . . . . . . . . . . . . . . . . . . . . . .

. . . . . . . . . . . . . . . . . . . . . . . . . . . . . . . . . . . . . . . . . . . . . . . . . . . . . . . .

. . . . . . . . . . . . . . . . . . . . . . . . . . . . . . . . . . . . . . . . . . . . . . . . . . . . . . . .

. . . . . . . . . . . . . . . . . . . . . . . . . . . . . . . . . . . . . . . . . . . . . . . . . . . . . . . .

. . . . . . . . . . . . . . . . . . . . . . . . . . . . . . . . . . . . . . . . . . . . . . . . . . . . . . . .

. . . . . . . . . . . . . . . . . . . . . . . . . . . . . . . . . . . . . . . . . . . . . . . . . . . . . . . .

## *Prayer for Today*

Father, I thank you for showing me there are no limits to how great I can be and how much progress I can make in my walk with You. Therefore, I refuse to be stagnant or live an average or mediocre life. I choose to always open my spirit to receive visions of progress, greatness and excellence and I receive the ability of the Spirit to function in these new and higher levels in the Name of Jesus. Amen.

# DAY 37
## Transform Me

*Create in me a clean heart, O God; and renew a right spirit within me.*
**— PSALM 51:10 NIV**

Jesus loves you! Unconditionally and always. He loves you just the way He finds you. PERIOD. You came to this chapter because the Holy Spirit put His finger on some issues that you have been dealing with in your life and brought them up into the light, and said, "This right here; it needs to change. Let Me change you here." You may not have recognized that's what He was doing, but that's why you're reading this right now.

That's a wonderful thing! Who wants to remain stuck? The Holy Spirit's work in your soul goes deep, healing your shame, cleansing your motivations, empowering new behaviors, writing a new chapter in your life, enabling you to experience the kind of intimacy God created you for. Jesus invites you to invite Him right into the middle of your story. This is not an arm's length transaction. No, He's right in the middle of your business, if you let Him in. You may have seen that old picture of Jesus knocking at the door. There's no doorknob on the outside; you have to let Him in. It's only then that He can change you from the inside out. Your role, most of all, is to just keep saying Yes! Each thing He brings up to you, just say Yes! Let Him do the rest!. Allow Him to deal with your "stuff." As long as you keep saying Yes, He won't stop until His good work in you is accomplished because He loves you too much to let you stay in that condition or in your stuff. He wants to change you, to grow you up, to make you more and more like Himself, to become the glorious human being He originally created you to be. That kind of transformation only happens from the inside out. And today is the perfect day for a transformation.

. . . . . . . . . . . . . . . . . . . . . . . . . . . . . . . . . . . . . . . . . . . . . . .

. . . . . . . . . . . . . . . . . . . . . . . . . . . . . . . . . . . . . . . . . . . . . . .

. . . . . . . . . . . . . . . . . . . . . . . . . . . . . . . . . . . . . . . . . . . . . . .

. . . . . . . . . . . . . . . . . . . . . . . . . . . . . . . . . . . . . . . . . . . . . . .

. . . . . . . . . . . . . . . . . . . . . . . . . . . . . . . . . . . . . . . . . . . . . . .

. . . . . . . . . . . . . . . . . . . . . . . . . . . . . . . . . . . . . . . . . . . . . . .

. . . . . . . . . . . . . . . . . . . . . . . . . . . . . . . . . . . . . . . . . . . . . . .

## Prayer for Today

Father God, thank You for showing me what true love looks like. Please perfect me in Your love by showing me the parts of my life that are not in line with Your Holy Spirit. Show me where I am selfish, self-serving, and easily angered, so that I can surrender those things to You and allow You to replace those traits with Your selfless love. Transform me into someone who loves others just like You love me. In Jesus' name, Amen.

# DAY 38
## Don't Settle

We who are strong ought to bear with the failings of the weak and not to please ourselves.
**– ROMANS 15:1 NIV**

Sadly, it is a common story in the Christian life that God calls us to something wonderful, but we settle for something mediocre along the way and run the risk of missing out on the great things God had planned for us. When God called Abraham, He told him to go "to the land I will show you" (Genesis 12:1). At the time, that land was called Canaan. But when Abraham first left Ur, the city of his birth, he only made it as far as Harran, which was a long way off from Canaan and far from God's best for him. The temptation to compromise and settle for less is something we all will face. When this temptation comes, we must stand strong on the promises of God. We miss out on God's best when we compromise with the world or take matters into our own hands. In Abraham's case, he believed he was honoring his father by settling in Harran. He also thought he was helping fulfill God's promise when he slept with Hagar. But thank the Lord for His graciousness! He didn't leave Abraham in his sin or forsake him because of his failures. The good news is that God will also do the same for us, no matter how we may have compromised. He stands ready to lead us to His perfect plan for our lives if only we will follow. So, remember don't ever let someone tell you that you can't do anything. Never live up to someone else's expectations of you because the only expectations that matter is what God wants for you and what He has provided for you in your life.

. . . . . . . . . . . . . . . . . . . . . . . . . . . . . . . . . . . . . . . . . . . . . . . . . . . . . . . . . .

. . . . . . . . . . . . . . . . . . . . . . . . . . . . . . . . . . . . . . . . . . . . . . . . . . . . . . . . . .

. . . . . . . . . . . . . . . . . . . . . . . . . . . . . . . . . . . . . . . . . . . . . . . . . . . . . . . . . .

. . . . . . . . . . . . . . . . . . . . . . . . . . . . . . . . . . . . . . . . . . . . . . . . . . . . . . . . . .

. . . . . . . . . . . . . . . . . . . . . . . . . . . . . . . . . . . . . . . . . . . . . . . . . . . . . . . . . .

. . . . . . . . . . . . . . . . . . . . . . . . . . . . . . . . . . . . . . . . . . . . . . . . . . . . . . . . . .

. . . . . . . . . . . . . . . . . . . . . . . . . . . . . . . . . . . . . . . . . . . . . . . . . . . . . . . . . .

## Prayer for Today

Lord, thank You that You will never forsake me and that You are working for my good and Your glory. Help me to obey Your will, remembering that You have great plans for my life. This I pray in the name of Jesus. Amen.

# Faith It Until You Make It

"The Lord is my shepherd; I have all that I need. He lets me rest in green meadows; he leads me beside peaceful streams. He renews my strength. He guides me along right paths, bringing honor to his name. Even when I walk through the darkest valley, I will not be afraid, for you are close beside me. Your rod and your staff protect and comfort me. You prepare a feast for me in the presence of my enemies. You honor me by anointing my head with oil. My cup overflows with blessings. Surely your goodness and unfailing love will pursue me all the days of my life, and I will live in the house of the Lord forever."

**– PSALMS 23 NLT**

There are many reasons I find myself afraid. Horror movies, snakes, rodents, my loved ones' safety, COVID-19, failing at something, rejection, what might happen tomorrow, the list could go on and on! I could occupy all of my thoughts with things that I am afraid of. It could quite literally be all-consuming. I know many people who are afraid. Those who don't know which way to turn next because life is so uncertain. Those who let fear consume their lives. I'll admit, I sometimes want to let it go. I want to stop doing all of the things that terrify me and live in a bubble. I want my worry, my anxiety, and my fear to be gone. However, that is not a reality. Even if I lived in a bubble, I am certain that I would find other things to worry about, that my fears and my anxieties would still consume me. I would still live in darkness. Instead of living in fear, God calls us to live in faith. That does not mean that we will never be afraid, but it means that when those fears come, we face them, we name them, and then we give them to God. It means that we ask God for help. God is so much bigger than any fear we face. Big or small, God is always greater. He is always there to stand by your side to help you face your fears and protect you in your weakest moments. He is so much stronger than any earthly thing. Remember that He has put you in this season for a reason and He will help you through it. Stay strong in your faith and He will always guide you. Remember that He is the creator of the universe and can make miracles happen and He can certainly help you work through your fears and difficult seasons of life.

· · · · · · · · · · · · · · · · · · · · · · · · · · · · · · · · · · · · · · · · · · · · · · · · · · · ·

· · · · · · · · · · · · · · · · · · · · · · · · · · · · · · · · · · · · · · · · · · · · · · · · · · · ·

· · · · · · · · · · · · · · · · · · · · · · · · · · · · · · · · · · · · · · · · · · · · · · · · · · · ·

· · · · · · · · · · · · · · · · · · · · · · · · · · · · · · · · · · · · · · · · · · · · · · · · · · · ·

· · · · · · · · · · · · · · · · · · · · · · · · · · · · · · · · · · · · · · · · · · · · · · · · · · · ·

· · · · · · · · · · · · · · · · · · · · · · · · · · · · · · · · · · · · · · · · · · · · · · · · · · · ·

· · · · · · · · · · · · · · · · · · · · · · · · · · · · · · · · · · · · · · · · · · · · · · · · · · · ·

## Prayer for Today

Lord, I am so needy for Your strength. I cannot do life with any measure of success without You. I look to You now and draw from the power that is mine to abolish any doubt or fear that I carry in my heart. I claim the victory that is mine today as I depend on You. Amen.

# DAY 40
## Bless YOUs

May the Lord bless you
and protect you.
May the Lord smile on you
and be gracious to you.
May the Lord show you his favor
and give you his peace.
**– NUMBERS 6:24-26**

ACHOO! That's the universal sound for a sneeze. You might sneeze because you have a cold. Or because dust, pet hair, or pollen is tickling inside your nose. Some people even sneeze when they step out into the sunlight! We use the word "bless you" a lot. "God bless you," is the common response you say to someone who is sneezing, or we might use it to end a conversation: "Well, it's really good to see you! God bless!" And sometimes we may hear people say, after something unexpected occurs, that this was a blessing or even state they have favor. God's ultimate blessing is the gift of His Son. Through faith in Christ's completed work, we receive God's forgiveness, righteousness, and His in-dwelling Holy Spirit, gifting us with His grace to restore peace, protection, and prosperity in every area of our life. Today, realize that God longs to bless you. The stresses of life experienced during these unprecedented times can have one feeling so challenged, overwhelmed and so broken. However, in all of this we recognize that God is not blind to our situations. God is all powerful and is able to do exceeding abundantly above all we may ask or think. The doors God chooses to open in our lives can leave us standing in awe. He also can close the doors that He feels would harm us or is not good for us. Be encouraged that the greatest blessings today may come from times of extreme testing. May the Lord Bless everything that your hands touch. May His fingerprint be on every assignment that you oversee. May you perform above and beyond the status quo. May you excel in all that you do. May He make your feet like hinds' feet and cause you to walk upon high places. May He stabilize you. May He comfort you. May He give you witty ideas to transform the hearts of generations. May you reach and impact cultures. May you shift environments. May you transform spaces and workplaces. May your light shine through witty ideas, inventions and processes. May your wise counsel far exceed the rest. It is then we experience that God will turn things around. He makes every crooked path straight. He is a Way Maker, Miracle Worker, light in the darkness. May God turn your mourning into dancing. May you experience His blessings while you continue reading this devotional journal with me.

*Day*

# 40

. . . . . . . . . . . . . . . . . . . . . . . . . . . . . . . . . . . . . . . . . . . . . . . . . . . . . . . . . . .

. . . . . . . . . . . . . . . . . . . . . . . . . . . . . . . . . . . . . . . . . . . . . . . . . . . . . . . . . . .

. . . . . . . . . . . . . . . . . . . . . . . . . . . . . . . . . . . . . . . . . . . . . . . . . . . . . . . . . . .

. . . . . . . . . . . . . . . . . . . . . . . . . . . . . . . . . . . . . . . . . . . . . . . . . . . . . . . . . . .

. . . . . . . . . . . . . . . . . . . . . . . . . . . . . . . . . . . . . . . . . . . . . . . . . . . . . . . . . . .

. . . . . . . . . . . . . . . . . . . . . . . . . . . . . . . . . . . . . . . . . . . . . . . . . . . . . . . . . . .

. . . . . . . . . . . . . . . . . . . . . . . . . . . . . . . . . . . . . . . . . . . . . . . . . . . . . . . . . . .

## Prayer for Today

Lord, help me receive Your blessings so I can be a blessing to others. Remove all selfish desires and help me grow in full humility and grace. I need You right now Lord to bless my coming and going, family, friends and those I may come in contact with on a daily basis. Show me your continuous mercy, in Jesus' name, Amen.

# Don't Throw in the Towel

Jesus answered, "It is written: 'Man shall not live on bread alone, but on every word that comes from the mouth of God.'"
**– MATTHEW 4:4 NIV**

The hard part when approaching a crossroad is choosing how you will respond. Numerous passages in the Bible connect the number 40 to periods of trial, testing, or hardship, however I want to focus on the number 41 which represents a beacon of hope for postponed dreams and promised lands. Amid the troubles of everyday life, it's almost as if 41 is shouting, "I got next!" During the 40 days after His resurrection, Jesus appeared to His disciples on several occasions—proving to them that He was alive and breathing new life into them as He explained the Kingdom of God and commissioned them to build it. On day 41, after promising to send the Holy Spirit in His place, He ascended into heaven, leaving the disciples to carry out His plan for launching the church—a church that, by the way, is still prevailing against the gates of hell. Whether you're stuck in the storms of life, in serious need of a second chance, stranded in the wilderness of unexpected circumstances or unfulfilled expectations, facing what seems to be an unbeatable giant or bearing up against unspeakable temptation, the pattern is clear. The number 41 represents the dawn of a new day—the hope and promise that if you don't quit, the rain will stop, the giant will fall and you will enter your "promised land." Identify your 41. On this day or within this month, what are you believing? Are you going to make it to day 41 and give up or are you going to keep pressing forward? The time is now and the decision is yours.

. . . . . . . . . . . . . . . . . . . . . . . . . . . . . . . . . . . . . . . . . . . . . . . . . . . . . . .

. . . . . . . . . . . . . . . . . . . . . . . . . . . . . . . . . . . . . . . . . . . . . . . . . . . . . . .

. . . . . . . . . . . . . . . . . . . . . . . . . . . . . . . . . . . . . . . . . . . . . . . . . . . . . . .

. . . . . . . . . . . . . . . . . . . . . . . . . . . . . . . . . . . . . . . . . . . . . . . . . . . . . . .

. . . . . . . . . . . . . . . . . . . . . . . . . . . . . . . . . . . . . . . . . . . . . . . . . . . . . . .

. . . . . . . . . . . . . . . . . . . . . . . . . . . . . . . . . . . . . . . . . . . . . . . . . . . . . . .

. . . . . . . . . . . . . . . . . . . . . . . . . . . . . . . . . . . . . . . . . . . . . . . . . . . . . . .

## Prayer for Today

Lord, I pray that You will rebuild my faith. Even at times when I don't see or experience the good things that You have in store for me. Help me to have a faith that is unshaken by my circumstances. I place my faith back in Jesus and to follow Him closely for the rest of my life. May this prayer become my reality in Jesus' name, Amen.

# Just Live

And let us not grow weary of doing good, for in due season we will reap, if we do not give up.
**— GALATIANS 6:9 NIV**

Are you tired of your life being dry, confused and without direction? Are you weary of having to strive for everything in life? Just remember, until you're able to get your well cleared out and unplugged, everything will be difficult, disappointing and unfulfilling. No matter what you try, you won't be able to taste the water from that river. And that water satisfies like nothing else. Remember, God put a river of life inside each of us. We just need to tap into that stream by clearing up what blocks its flow. We desperately need God every day, to bring joy and hope to our own lives and to those around us. Without Him, we will most certainly run dry. For we're not meant to run on our own. Our strength can't carry us through every hard struggle and hardship we may encounter. But He promises rest and peace for our souls even in the midst of weariness and burdens.

God can help you forgive, see the needs of those around you, and let go of past hurts or wrongs. He wants to help you deal with the "stones" and "debris" that are stopping up your well. Make a choice today to stop spending your life fighting, struggling and trudging through the mud with every step. Stop taking inventory of what you've lost and take a good look at what you've got left. Ask God to help you clear out the debris and stop living by feelings and start living by faith.

. . . . . . . . . . . . . . . . . . . . . . . . . . . . . . . . . . . . . . . . . . . . . . . . . . .

. . . . . . . . . . . . . . . . . . . . . . . . . . . . . . . . . . . . . . . . . . . . . . . . . . .

. . . . . . . . . . . . . . . . . . . . . . . . . . . . . . . . . . . . . . . . . . . . . . . . . . .

. . . . . . . . . . . . . . . . . . . . . . . . . . . . . . . . . . . . . . . . . . . . . . . . . . .

. . . . . . . . . . . . . . . . . . . . . . . . . . . . . . . . . . . . . . . . . . . . . . . . . . .

. . . . . . . . . . . . . . . . . . . . . . . . . . . . . . . . . . . . . . . . . . . . . . . . . . .

## Prayer for Today

Dear God, thank You that Your yoke is easy and Your burden is light. Thank You that You promise to give the worried, the hurried, the pressured and stressed out rest and peace for our souls if we'll just come before You. Thank You that You already know all that concerns us, and You care. We're so grateful for Your reminder that we don't have to carry it all on our own. Forgive us for the times that we've tried to fix things in our own power, for not taking the time to rest, or coming to You first with our needs and burdens. Thank You for the refreshing that comes from Your Spirit, filling us with joy, covering us with a shield, leading us forward with hope. Equip us to be those who take notice of others who seem weary and burdened too. Help us to slow down, to take the time, to point others to You. In Jesus' name, Amen.

# It's Worth The Wait

So now, come back to your God. Act with love and justice, and always depend on him.
**– HOSEA 12:6 NLT**

All of us are waiting for something. On this side of heaven there will persist a nagging sense of lack. Whether you're longing for a husband, a baby, a sense of purpose, a pain-free body or cure, prosperity, or simply change, an ache can well up in our soul.

And yet God's Word says: "The Lord is my shepherd, I shall not want." Psalm 23:1

Days after not getting the promotion I wanted so badly I remember coming across these verses: "The Lord is good to those who wait for him, to the soul who seeks him. It is good that one should wait quietly for the salvation of the Lord." Lamentations 3:25-26. I realized that's what I was doing – waiting. But there was more to it. I needed to wait upon God, to wait for Him to act. In this case, I had to trust God's timing. I know how not being where you thought you would be can make you feel defeated. It can make you feel small, inadequate, insignificant and unworthy, but sometimes you being delayed, rejected or denied just means you're still being prepared and positioned for greater and better. There will be some paths you take that are so significant that will require some preheating or preparation. In the wait there will come strength and courage. I urge you to review the truths in Psalm 27 each time you are tempted to be afraid. Don't become paralyzed and ineffective. Take yourself out of the grind of fear! Look upon each threatening circumstance as an opportunity to grow in your faith, rather than to retreat. How? Follow David's example. First, call to mind what you know to be true about God. Secondly, express what you need boldly. Lastly, wait. Let the fearful circumstance become God's opportunity to strengthen you. So trust the process because while you're working and preparing God is still working. Nothing is impossible with God. God knows all things. God sees everything upon the earth. The wisest of men are fools compared to Him and His matchless wisdom. These facts – that God is the omnipotent, omniscient, omnipresent, wise King – can settle our hearts with peace.

It's not that He can't do what we're waiting for, it's that He knows the perfect time and way to do it.

· · · · · · · · · · · · · · · · · · · · · · · · · · · · · · · · · · · · · · · · · · · · · · · · · ·

· · · · · · · · · · · · · · · · · · · · · · · · · · · · · · · · · · · · · · · · · · · · · · · · · ·

· · · · · · · · · · · · · · · · · · · · · · · · · · · · · · · · · · · · · · · · · · · · · · · · · ·

· · · · · · · · · · · · · · · · · · · · · · · · · · · · · · · · · · · · · · · · · · · · · · · · · ·

· · · · · · · · · · · · · · · · · · · · · · · · · · · · · · · · · · · · · · · · · · · · · · · · · ·

· · · · · · · · · · · · · · · · · · · · · · · · · · · · · · · · · · · · · · · · · · · · · · · · · ·

· · · · · · · · · · · · · · · · · · · · · · · · · · · · · · · · · · · · · · · · · · · · · · · · · ·

## *Prayer for Today*

Father, many plans are in my heart, but I pray that Your purpose prevails. Let Your will be done in my life and let the plans that You have released in heaven, be aligned here on earth. I pray that I understand Your purpose for me so that I do not stray from it or forget it. Let my desires become aligned with Your purpose so that I am not conflicted in my lifestyle. This is the prayer of my heart. In Jesus' name, Amen.

# DAY 44
## Go

*But blessed are those who trust in the Lord and have made the Lord their hope and confidence.*
**— JEREMIAH 17:7 NIV**

The word "go" is a small two letter word that carries tremendous power and authority. Did you know the word "go" is in the Bible over 1542 times and the word "stay" is in the Bible 62 times. Just doing the simple math here, the word "go" is mentioned over 1480 more times. I heard years ago from a famous preacher that the word "go" may be one of God's favorite commands. Have you ever felt like God was calling you to move? It may be to another job or to an entirely different state or country. Maybe you're being pulled in a particular direction as well? What do you do? Do you pack up and move? Just imagine, you've become comfortable in your home; your children are attending great schools, you have a stable income and then all of a sudden you get this sudden urge to leave your beautiful suburban life and become a full-time missionary overseas. Or maybe your back and forth conversations with God sound like this,"God, I just got here, I just got the promotion and now making six figures for the first time. The kids are thriving in their schools. God I got a great thing going right now." So as the control freak you may be, or maybe I'm describing myself here. You stop moving and by your lack of movement you silenced God and turned up the voice of the enemy. But hey Sis, could it be that God is just answering your prayers that you have been sending up for years but because it wasn't done in your specific timing, you have forgotten the prayer and now you are not ready for the God ordained relocation? Well, honey your timing is not God's timing.

Well, consider on Day 44, I am serving you an eviction notice on behalf of the Most High. God knows our future and there are times He just has to remove us willingly or not from our comfort zones. But know this, the more we practice faith, trust and obedience to God the more we will be able to discern His direction. There will come a time, and most likely many times when the Lord will come to us and simply say, "Go." There are specific places God wants us to be at certain times so that He can use us-- and even bless us--in ways that are specific to that particular location. Right now, I feel compelled to say, it's time to be in the right place, at the right time to receive the right portion of the blessing you have been praying for. When God asks us to move, He never asks us to go alone. He asks us to move because He wants to go somewhere and He wants us to move with Him! You don't have to make any decision all alone. Before hitting your head against the wall and beating yourself up with negative statements, seek guidance and listen, yes listen for the quiet voice of the Lord. And remember that God's command to GO does not always involve physically moving. Sometimes it may mean stepping up and not going somewhere. It might mean refusing to go to a party where drugs, drinking, and other forms of compromise will be taking place. Maybe it means, not putting in for a dream job or the job you thought was your dream because it would mean that your work hours would conflict with your worship hours. It might even mean declining acceptance into a college that would transplant you right into party central itself but deciding to attend a local community college first to obtain your general education requirements while saving money living with your parents.

When God sees you, He sees greatness, purpose and unlimited potential. God's grace and favor in your life enables you to become what He sees. But first, you have to open your heart and take the limits off of your life and move when God says move. God desires to use you. Because God does not see us the way we view ourselves, especially on our worst days, it's important to remember that He always has a purpose for us. Christianity is about moving away from the self into self-less loving. So, when God tells you to GO, you don't need to get ready, you just need to GO in Jesus name!

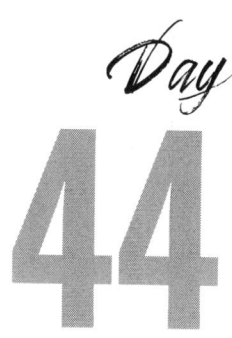

Day

44

. . . . . . . . . . . . . . . . . . . . . . . . . . . . . . . . . . . . . . . . . . . . . . . . . . . . . .

. . . . . . . . . . . . . . . . . . . . . . . . . . . . . . . . . . . . . . . . . . . . . . . . . . . . . .

. . . . . . . . . . . . . . . . . . . . . . . . . . . . . . . . . . . . . . . . . . . . . . . . . . . . . .

. . . . . . . . . . . . . . . . . . . . . . . . . . . . . . . . . . . . . . . . . . . . . . . . . . . . . .

. . . . . . . . . . . . . . . . . . . . . . . . . . . . . . . . . . . . . . . . . . . . . . . . . . . . . .

. . . . . . . . . . . . . . . . . . . . . . . . . . . . . . . . . . . . . . . . . . . . . . . . . . . . . .

. . . . . . . . . . . . . . . . . . . . . . . . . . . . . . . . . . . . . . . . . . . . . . . . . . . . . .

## Prayer for Today

Lord, I pray for courage to walk in the plans that You have for me. I pray that You would keep me close as I step out in faith and do Your will for my life. I admit I am afraid, but I will not let fear rob me from the blessings that You have for me. Give me peace, confidence, and courage in Your name I pray, Amen!

# DAY 45
# Strength of A Woman

Don't be afraid, for I am with you. Don't be discouraged, for I am your God. I will strengthen you and help you. I will hold you up with my victorious right hand.
**— ISAIAH 41:10 NLT**

The world we live in has sold us a bundle of lies about our gender and what constitutes strength. I for one am sick of it. In my younger years I bought into all of it so quickly that I am embarrassed. Not even thinking to check it against what God has to say. I was a smart woman; I thought I knew what it meant to be strong. I really had no clue.

When a woman was cheated on by her husband I would side with the throng shouting, "Leave that unfaithful jerk." Until that woman was me after 8 years of marriage. Although we are now celebrating almost 26 years of marriage, we lived a double life that involved an infidelity story and even more shocking reconciliation. A story of staying and not leaving. A story of a couple renewed and redeemed by the power of Christ alone. A victory story ordained by God. It was only by the grace of God allowing us to be under Christian care and therapy and recommitment to allow the overhaul to take place. Let me say this very clearly, infidelity happens way before the actual act of cheating. However, since that time of healing, I am now able to share my testimony with others without shame and embarrassment and am now able to walk with others who have gone through that same type of pain but have chosen to stay married. In my marriage I saw the miracle of reconciliation as God turned my anger and resentment towards my husband to passion. I saw how the Holy Spirit restored peace in our home and drove my husband towards repentance and a renewed commitment to run after God. Going through and healing from brokenness brought about strength I never knew I possessed. Not so many years ago, my mental picture of a strong woman was one with ambition, who had a successful career and took care of her family. Someone who had it all together and worked hard to accomplish her dreams. Now having walked with women who struggle with anxiety, wrestle with depression and deal with chronic emotional pain, I see real strength. These same women call on God for help, trusting in Him to carry them on. They pick themselves up and walk out their doors to face a harsh world that they don't seem to fit into. Despite the enemy's attacks, they keep getting back up and loving on others. They worship with passion and praise with joy. Doing battle bravely with the sword of God's Word.

The career woman can be a strong woman in Christ, but she is also the woman who gives up her worldly status to stay home and raise her children. She is the one who stands up and says "No" to the teaching of the world when everyone else is saying, "Okay, I guess, whatever." She is the one who picks up her Bible to read instead of the latest trending novel. She is the one loving the unlovable and forgiving the unforgivable. She is the one who works hard at pleasing her Lord even if that displeases the world around her. Ladies, don't eat up the lies the world is trying to push down your throat. You know deep in your heart that God's way always has been and always will be the best way. His opinion is the only one that matters. Show true strength in this world; admire true strength in this world. Be determined to walk that narrow path of truth while others carouse down easy streets. If you have been living with a misunderstanding of strength, it's time to take a stand and get it right. Hear God's word today and let this be your prayer right now:

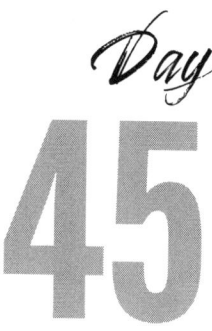

## Day 45

. . . . . . . . . . . . . . . . . . . . . . . . . . . . . . . . . . . . . . . . . . . . . . . . . . . . . . . . . . . . . . . . .

. . . . . . . . . . . . . . . . . . . . . . . . . . . . . . . . . . . . . . . . . . . . . . . . . . . . . . . . . . . . . . . . .

. . . . . . . . . . . . . . . . . . . . . . . . . . . . . . . . . . . . . . . . . . . . . . . . . . . . . . . . . . . . . . . . .

. . . . . . . . . . . . . . . . . . . . . . . . . . . . . . . . . . . . . . . . . . . . . . . . . . . . . . . . . . . . . . . . .

. . . . . . . . . . . . . . . . . . . . . . . . . . . . . . . . . . . . . . . . . . . . . . . . . . . . . . . . . . . . . . . . .

. . . . . . . . . . . . . . . . . . . . . . . . . . . . . . . . . . . . . . . . . . . . . . . . . . . . . . . . . . . . . . . . .

. . . . . . . . . . . . . . . . . . . . . . . . . . . . . . . . . . . . . . . . . . . . . . . . . . . . . . . . . . . . . . . . .

### Prayer for Today

Holy Spirit teach me Your way and help me walk in spirit and truth. Heal my brokenness and make me whole again. In Jesus' name, Amen.

# DAY 46
## Nope, Not Today!

*And we know that for those who love God all things work together for good, for those who are called according to his purpose.*
**– ROMANS 8:28 ESV**

It's clear that in life we all will experience many uncontrollable challenges on a daily basis and some are greater than others. Our lives have many facets with work, home, family, friends, colleagues, partners and perhaps children as well. And over the years, no doubt, commitments have crept in, almost unnoticed, to the point where, whether you know it or not, there are probably multiple versions of you juggling lots of different plates. During the time that I started writing this book, I changed jobs twice yet within the same organization and there have been several times when the feeling of being overwhelmed has crept in like a dark shadow. But, it doesn't have to be that way if you know how to control the controllables. For this moment, think about how many versions of you there are. There's the personal you with family and friends, the professional you with colleagues and bosses, you in a relationship, you as a parent, as well as just you being you. Each version of you has to meet different demands and expectations. Each version of you dialed up or down as you and your life evolve.

Managing the tensions between these various versions of me is something I've had to learn and, if I'm candid, am still learning, as new demands and challenges arise. The answer isn't to become universally excellent at all of them, but to understand which one requires the most attention at any given point. Remember, there are many versions of you but only one physical you. One thing I learned is the value of saying no because every time you say 'yes' to something unimportant, you are saying 'no' to something important. Remember you can't be all things to all people. Know your priorities. Know your goals. Know what needs to get done over the coming weeks, months and years for you to feel that you have played your best game. And, say 'no' to everything else.

Sure, some people around you might not be happy. But would you rather live your life according to the approval, rules and demands of others, or be aligned with your truth, your dreams and your goals?

What are you going to say 'no' to today, tomorrow, next week and next month, to ensure you achieve personal and professional success?

. . . . . . . . . . . . . . . . . . . . . . . . . . . . . . . . . . . . . . . . . . . . . . . . . . . . . . . . . . . . .

. . . . . . . . . . . . . . . . . . . . . . . . . . . . . . . . . . . . . . . . . . . . . . . . . . . . . . . . . . . . .

. . . . . . . . . . . . . . . . . . . . . . . . . . . . . . . . . . . . . . . . . . . . . . . . . . . . . . . . . . . . .

. . . . . . . . . . . . . . . . . . . . . . . . . . . . . . . . . . . . . . . . . . . . . . . . . . . . . . . . . . . . .

. . . . . . . . . . . . . . . . . . . . . . . . . . . . . . . . . . . . . . . . . . . . . . . . . . . . . . . . . . . . .

. . . . . . . . . . . . . . . . . . . . . . . . . . . . . . . . . . . . . . . . . . . . . . . . . . . . . . . . . . . . .

. . . . . . . . . . . . . . . . . . . . . . . . . . . . . . . . . . . . . . . . . . . . . . . . . . . . . . . . . . . . .

## Prayer for Today

Heavenly Father, as we begin to take steps in the direction of our purpose, we ask that You give us wisdom, insight and patience. We ask in faith that as Your word promises us, that You will give us wisdom in every small and big decision as we further step into our purpose. In Jesus' name, Amen.

# Water Walkers

"Come," he said. Then Peter got down out of the boat, walked on the water and came toward Jesus.
But when he saw the wind, he was afraid
and, beginning to sink, cried out, "Lord, save me!"
— **MATTHEW 14: 29-30 NIV**

What does it take to have the kind of faith that Peter had to step out of the boat and to walk on the water? When we read this passage, we sometimes see the Peter that did not focus on Christ and began to sink. However, there was the other Peter. The one that had the courage and bravery to actually step out of the boat. As we study Peter, we see a disciple that wavered in his faith at times. He was passionate, but also uncontrollable in his emotions. In this moment of stepping out of the boat, he showed his passion and his boldness in getting to God. He was the only disciple that even thought about stepping out of the boat. However, when he took his eyes off Jesus, he began to sink. When you can't change your circumstances, change your concentration. Peter walked on water until his concentration broke (Matthew 14:22-33). Once he took his eyes off Jesus and saw the wind and the waves, he began to sink. Likewise, if you concentrate on your circumstances, your soul will sink. But if you can concentrate on the Creator, fixing your eyes on Jesus and all that you have to be grateful for, you can rise above any situation.

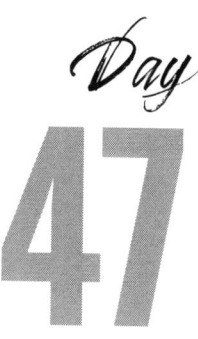
· · · · · · · · · · · · · · · · · · · · · · · · · · · · · · · · · · · · · · · · · · · · · · · · · · · · · · · · · · · ·

· · · · · · · · · · · · · · · · · · · · · · · · · · · · · · · · · · · · · · · · · · · · · · · · · · · · · · · · · · · ·

· · · · · · · · · · · · · · · · · · · · · · · · · · · · · · · · · · · · · · · · · · · · · · · · · · · · · · · · · · · ·

· · · · · · · · · · · · · · · · · · · · · · · · · · · · · · · · · · · · · · · · · · · · · · · · · · · · · · · · · · · ·

· · · · · · · · · · · · · · · · · · · · · · · · · · · · · · · · · · · · · · · · · · · · · · · · · · · · · · · · · · · ·

· · · · · · · · · · · · · · · · · · · · · · · · · · · · · · · · · · · · · · · · · · · · · · · · · · · · · · · · · · · ·

· · · · · · · · · · · · · · · · · · · · · · · · · · · · · · · · · · · · · · · · · · · · · · · · · · · · · · · · · · · ·

## Prayer for Today

Gracious and Holy Father, give us the wisdom to discover You, the intelligence to understand You, the diligence to seek after You, the patience to wait for You,

eyes to behold You, a heart to meditate upon You, and a life to proclaim You,

through the power of the Spirit of Jesus, our Lord. Amen.

# Crave God Like Chips

Taste and see that the Lord is good. Oh, the joys of those who take refuge in him.
**—PSALM 34:8 NIV**

I knew I was in trouble when I found myself looking at the back of the package, mentally calculating how many calories I would consume if I ended up eating the entire bag of Doritos. The total was at least enough to keep me from finishing it off or maybe it was the gut ache I was starting to feel. They shouldn't be allowed to make food like this, it is so hard to stop. Pair it with a Coke Zero and I'm not sure life could get much better. Plus it's cheap. Like a bag of happiness for only $2 – what a deal! But then the thought came: What if only I craved God as much as I craved junk food? This may sound silly, but oh how it cut my heart deep. Ladies, have you had a similar thought? "If only I craved God as much as I crave (fill in the blank)." Fill in the blank with whatever you desire: your Boo, your favorite TV series, pumpkin spice anything, money, wine, beauty, a baby, comfort, career or chocolate, etc.

We spend our lives running after what our flesh craves and desires. We throw our money, time and efforts at these things. And why not? Many of them come cheap and easy! Like Doritos on a shelf at the store for only $2 a bag. We can just turn on the TV, buy more clothes, hit the coffee shop, pop a bottle, or go through the fast food drive-thru. Happy and satisfied...until... tomorrow. Then we find ourselves back in line, making more purchases or searching for new thrills. I don't want to live that way! And the Bible tells me I shouldn't. As Christians, we have been set free from the bondage of sin. It no longer has a hold of you, so you no longer have to cater to the demands of your flesh. "Let not sin therefore reign in your mortal body, to make you obey its passions. For sin will have no dominion over you, since you are not under law but under grace." Roman 6:12-14. Thinking of Doritos having dominion over me sounds silly, but when I give in to this type of temptation that is exactly what I am allowing. That is awful. My heart's desire is to crave God more than anything else. I want to yearn for Him above all temporary pleasures. I want Psalm 42:1-2 to describe me, "As a deer pants for flowing streams, so pants my soul for you, O God. My soul thirsts for God, for the living God." I want God alone to have dominion over my attentions and affections.

So how do we make this happen? I think Psalm 34:8 is fitting, "Oh, taste and see that the Lord is good! Blessed is the man who takes refuge in Him!" The answer is to consume more of God so we can comprehend more of His goodness. When we understand more about our amazing God, our faith increases and our hope is established in Him. We take refuge in Him like the Psalm says and not worldly pleasures. Then we can say, "How sweet are Your words to my taste! Yes, sweeter than honey to my mouth!" Psalm 119:103. The result is an increased desire for more! This is a good craving, a holy craving. One you are encouraged to indulge in daily and eternally. So turn away from whatever it is your flesh is screaming for and set your heart on pursuing more of God. "For He satisfies the longing soul, and the hungry soul He fills with good things." Psalm 107:9. It's not too late. Time to get back to strength training on the word of God. Pray for a hunger for the spiritual. The cure is double – when we have more of God, our souls are satisfied and the cravings of the flesh are stilled. So taste and see that the Lord is good today, open up his Word and find your satisfaction in it.

. . . . . . . . . . . . . . . . . . . . . . . . . . . . . . . . . . . . . . . . . . . .

. . . . . . . . . . . . . . . . . . . . . . . . . . . . . . . . . . . . . . . . . . . .

. . . . . . . . . . . . . . . . . . . . . . . . . . . . . . . . . . . . . . . . . . . .

. . . . . . . . . . . . . . . . . . . . . . . . . . . . . . . . . . . . . . . . . . . .

. . . . . . . . . . . . . . . . . . . . . . . . . . . . . . . . . . . . . . . . . . . .

. . . . . . . . . . . . . . . . . . . . . . . . . . . . . . . . . . . . . . . . . . . .

. . . . . . . . . . . . . . . . . . . . . . . . . . . . . . . . . . . . . . . . . . . .

## Prayer for Today

Dear God, Please help me gain self control over my desire for food. I do not want food to fill my empty emotional and physical void. Please help me to make healthier choices and turn away from foods that do not support positive health for this wonderful body You have given me. Please help me to love myself as You love me and to take care of my body as You take care of me. Please help me to love myself for who I am and accept that I need your help to change my life. I pray that I can learn to love and respect my body so that I am healthy for myself and family. In Jesus name, Amen.

# DAY 49
## Seriously Speaking

For I could wish that I myself were accursed and cut off from Christ for the sake of my brothers, my kinsmen according to the flesh.

**– ROMANS 9:3 NIV**

Do you have unsaved family members? I know many who have straddled the fence for years. If you're like me, you have prayed for their salvation and have asked others to do the same. We think about them once in a while and pray for them as we shake our heads wondering why they just don't get it. Not long ago I was driving down the road, once again praying for my lost family, just nonchalantly mentioning their names to God and I felt myself being frustrated with Him for not acting, not showing any movement in their lives at all. What is God waiting for? "Do a work in their heart and save them already!" I began to get so frustrated at God, begging Him to do something to change their hearts and desires. I remember the question coming back at me hitting me like a brick. "How serious are you? You barely bow your head as you ask Me to move in the lives of the people you say you love. You spend more time and money on your own pleasures than on ministering to those you claim to love. You say you love My word, but have not yet put these Words of Life into the hands of those that are lost. You tell Me to do something? How bad do you really want this?" No, God did not speak these words to me, but he was certainly doing heart surgery on me at that moment. He was cutting me deep and it hurt. Seriously speaking, there is often pain in hearing the truth. What work have I done or sacrifices have I made to encourage my lost family toward Christ? Very little. The apostle Paul was willing to give everything up to save those he loved, even his own salvation! He had "great sorrow and unceasing anguish" in his heart for them. Oftentimes the work that needs to be done before God opens the heart of someone to believe is the work that needs completed in us. Sometimes God lingers and delays breakthroughs in others so that He can teach and refine us first. Start with changing your approach and invest in serious intercessory prayer for your unsaved family members and friends. Ain't nobody got time for sugar coating prayers and avoiding the uncomfortable. If your loved ones are unsaved, they are on the burn list. Go back to your prayer closet and start with praying, fasting and getting back into the word. No matter what, start sending daily scriptures, messages and motivational quotes. You need to fight for them like them and your life is dependent on them being saved. How serious are you? How bad do you want it? If you have loved ones who are walking toward Hell and currently stand condemned, I encourage you to decide that now is the time to get serious and be bold, share Christ with them and pray for them like never before because this is a serious matter!

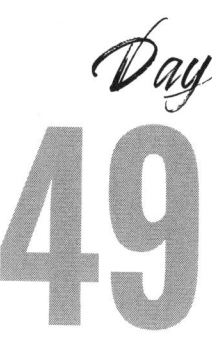

· · · · · · · · · · · · · · · · · · · · · · · · · · · · · · · · · · · · · · · · · · · · · · · · ·

· · · · · · · · · · · · · · · · · · · · · · · · · · · · · · · · · · · · · · · · · · · · · · · · ·

· · · · · · · · · · · · · · · · · · · · · · · · · · · · · · · · · · · · · · · · · · · · · · · · ·

· · · · · · · · · · · · · · · · · · · · · · · · · · · · · · · · · · · · · · · · · · · · · · · · ·

· · · · · · · · · · · · · · · · · · · · · · · · · · · · · · · · · · · · · · · · · · · · · · · · ·

· · · · · · · · · · · · · · · · · · · · · · · · · · · · · · · · · · · · · · · · · · · · · · · · ·

· · · · · · · · · · · · · · · · · · · · · · · · · · · · · · · · · · · · · · · · · · · · · · · · ·

## Prayer for Today

Dear Jesus, my mind can't seem to settle down and just live for today. Please help me find joy in my surroundings and contentment with my circumstances. Whatever is happening and wherever I am, I want to be completely satisfied and fulfilled, so I'm not constantly yearning for more or something different. I need You near me each moment, so joy can consume my spirit. For without You, there is no contentment with life, and there is no joy to light up my soul. I ask these things in Your precious name. Amen.

# Jericho Must Fall

When the trumpets sounded, the people shouted, and at the sound of the trumpet, when the men gave a loud shout, the wall collapsed; so everyone charged straight in, and they took the city.

**– JOSHUA 6:20 NIV**

Can I make a confession? Sometimes I quit way too soon. Is that you too?

There are times when I've grown tired of the struggle, and even tired of trying without experiencing any lasting results. And unfortunately, I have missed so many blessings and opportunities because I threw up my hands way too soon in the battle and said, "Just forget it, I'm done, I'm not capable or even worthy!" But for many of us, there are times when we're doing everything we know how to do and even have a support system to provide guidance but we still fall short in our relationships, our careers, our health, and often in our walk with God. But think about this, the Israelites walked around Jericho for six days, and as far as they could tell, nothing happened. I'm sure it unnerved the people behind the wall, but as far as the walkers could tell, not even one brick fell. What if they threw in the towel on the sixth lap and stopped walking and believing because they were just tired of going through the motions without experiencing results? It would have been easy for them to stop because after several laps around the wall, their current circumstance clearly indicated that nothing was going to happen. However, we know how the story ends. These faithful men and women continued to press forward and believed by faith that something was about to change and shift in the atmosphere. These faithful marchers didn't stop even when they didn't see the results after several laps because as they were marching, not only were they becoming physically stronger, their faith muscles were also strengthening along the way. Just like those faithful men and women, you can do the same. You're too close to stop now! Time to take one more step, one more swing at it, one more pitch of your brilliant ideas, because you might be just a few steps shy of experiencing your unbelievable and unfathomable breakthrough because you're already in close proximity of your next blessing. Declare to yourself that "in Jesus' name my walls of insecurity and uncertainty are coming down, right now and in this season!" It's time to get your megaphone or like the Isaelities your trumpet and shout! For the Lord has given you this moment, this opportunity, this new beginning and dominion over every area of your life.

· · · · · · · · · · · · · · · · · · · · · · · · · · · · · · · · · · · · · · · · · · · · · · · · · ·

· · · · · · · · · · · · · · · · · · · · · · · · · · · · · · · · · · · · · · · · · · · · · · · · · ·

· · · · · · · · · · · · · · · · · · · · · · · · · · · · · · · · · · · · · · · · · · · · · · · · · ·

· · · · · · · · · · · · · · · · · · · · · · · · · · · · · · · · · · · · · · · · · · · · · · · · · ·

· · · · · · · · · · · · · · · · · · · · · · · · · · · · · · · · · · · · · · · · · · · · · · · · · ·

· · · · · · · · · · · · · · · · · · · · · · · · · · · · · · · · · · · · · · · · · · · · · · · · · ·

· · · · · · · · · · · · · · · · · · · · · · · · · · · · · · · · · · · · · · · · · · · · · · · · · ·

## Prayer for Today

Help me Lord, to give control of my life over to You in every way, and to become the person You would have me be. Thank You Lord, that You have not given up on me and I ask You to teach me Your way from this day forward. In Jesus' name I pray, Amen.

# Let Your Light Shine

You are the light of the world. A town built on a hill cannot be hidden. Neither do people light a lamp and put it under a bowl. Instead they put it on its stand, and it gives light to everyone in the house. In the same way, let your light shine before others, that they may see your good deeds and glorify your Father in heaven.

**— MATTHEW 5:14-16 NIV**

The other night I walked into our very dark living room. I quickly found the lamp, and reached to turn it on. Immediately a warm glow radiated, lighting up the entire room and I began to recall the scripture in Matthew encouraging us to be the light of the world. Everyone goes through times in life that seem dark or heavy. You may be going through something right now, and you don't see how it could ever work out. You don't have the funds. Your relationships are struggling. Your career is at a dead-end. The problems look insurmountable. But if you will stay breakthrough–minded and focused on what God can do, you will begin to experience God's grace and mercy through His promises and light that will begin to burst through your darkness. Notice, it's not going to trickle in. It's not going to barely get there. No, like a flood, like the breaking forth of waters, it will come bursting in. That means, suddenly, things will change in your favor. Jesus tells us that we are the light of the world. The light within us is His light, the indwelling Christ, the Holy Spirit. What a special gift we possess! In Matthew 5:14-16, the scripture instructs us not to hide our light, but to let our light shine before others. One of the best ways to shine our light forward is through our good works. I am a firm believer that actions speak louder than words. We need to lead lives as people who have been redeemed by the Savior! When things seem dark, don't start complaining. Jesus is the light of the world which gives light to everyone. This means that He would be the one to drive away the darkness of the dominion of satan. This means that the truth would prevail upon deception. This also means that what is hidden and secret, will be made known to all. Jesus is the light that makes sense of the world. The darkness sought to put out the light from the time of His birth when Herod decreed the death of all boys of the same age in order to kill the Messiah before He could grow up and take Herod's kingdom away. The darkness overcame Adam and Eve in the Garden of Eden, bringing the influence of darkness upon the whole world. But it did not ever overcome the light of Jesus Christ. The darkness never prevailed against Him in his life, and it was defeated definitively by His death on the cross. Jesus is the Way and Truth and Light and He has prevailed. When you walk with God, you're walking in His light! Get back on that lamp stand, so your light can shine before others. Let Your Light Shine!

. . . . . . . . . . . . . . . . . . . . . . . . . . . . . . . . . . . . . . . . . . . . . . . . . . . . . . . . .

. . . . . . . . . . . . . . . . . . . . . . . . . . . . . . . . . . . . . . . . . . . . . . . . . . . . . . . . .

. . . . . . . . . . . . . . . . . . . . . . . . . . . . . . . . . . . . . . . . . . . . . . . . . . . . . . . . .

. . . . . . . . . . . . . . . . . . . . . . . . . . . . . . . . . . . . . . . . . . . . . . . . . . . . . . . . .

. . . . . . . . . . . . . . . . . . . . . . . . . . . . . . . . . . . . . . . . . . . . . . . . . . . . . . . . .

. . . . . . . . . . . . . . . . . . . . . . . . . . . . . . . . . . . . . . . . . . . . . . . . . . . . . . . . .

. . . . . . . . . . . . . . . . . . . . . . . . . . . . . . . . . . . . . . . . . . . . . . . . . . . . . . . . .

## *Prayer for Today*

Heavenly Father, I pray Matthew 5:14-16 over my life. Let me never forget I am the light of the world. It is my desire to shine brightly before others, allowing my attitude, words and actions to reflect the values of Jesus. I want my life to be a testimony to Your goodness. I pray that You would use me to spread light to those in need and that all my good deeds will glorify You. In Jesus' name, Amen.

# Have You Tried Prayer?

Never stop praying
**—1 THESSALONIANS 5:17 NLT**

The prayer of a righteous person has great power as it is working." James 5:16b. "Pray without ceasing," 1 Thessalonians 5:17. These are the two verses that have been ringing in my head for quite some time. It has been a week full of prayer needs and I am feeling the weight of this awesome gift God has given us. With the knowledge that we have around the clock, immediate access to God (because of what Jesus Christ did on the cross), why would we ever want to stop? As Christians we have the ear of the Almighty and He tells us that our prayers have great power. Why, because He is a Great God and His Holy Spirit dwells within us. Scripture also reminds us in Matthew 7:7 to, "Ask, and it will be given to you; seek, and you will find; knock, and it will be opened to you." Do you need any more convincing? If so, read Philippians 4:6, John 15:7, Mark 11:24, Colossians 4:2, Romans 8:26, Luke 11:9, Ephesians 6:18, and the list goes on and on.

I want to encourage you to pray more often and even pray in the moment. Don't wait for a less busy time because there never will be. Don't wait until you think of the right words. Don't wait until "later". Talking to the Alpha and Omega is of utmost importance and a number one priority. So prove it in your life. Pray for your neighbor with cancer, pray for the busy mom you know who is struggling, pray for your children and their friends and pray for whoever God places on your mind. Ok, pause for a second. Who was the first person that came to mind? Ok, pray for them too. Oftentimes when we tell someone that we will pray for them and we forget or get distracted. So, starting today, if and when you receive a prayer request, pray right there in the moment. Create a healthy habit within your family by seeking God first before all other personal needs. Make it a daily lifestyle as much as eating or talking together. Talk to God first. Let the conversation between you and your Heavenly Father flourish and become a continuous dialogue. After all, that's one reason it's called a relationship.

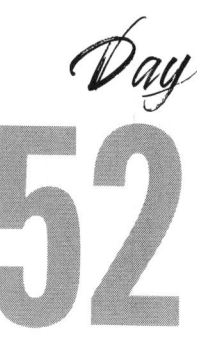

*Day*

# 52

. . . . . . . . . . . . . . . . . . . . . . . . . . . . . . . . . . . . . . . . . . . . . . . . . . . . . . . . . . . . . . . . . . . . . . . . . . . .

. . . . . . . . . . . . . . . . . . . . . . . . . . . . . . . . . . . . . . . . . . . . . . . . . . . . . . . . . . . . . . . . . . . . . . . . . . . .

. . . . . . . . . . . . . . . . . . . . . . . . . . . . . . . . . . . . . . . . . . . . . . . . . . . . . . . . . . . . . . . . . . . . . . . . . . . .

. . . . . . . . . . . . . . . . . . . . . . . . . . . . . . . . . . . . . . . . . . . . . . . . . . . . . . . . . . . . . . . . . . . . . . . . . . . .

. . . . . . . . . . . . . . . . . . . . . . . . . . . . . . . . . . . . . . . . . . . . . . . . . . . . . . . . . . . . . . . . . . . . . . . . . . . .

. . . . . . . . . . . . . . . . . . . . . . . . . . . . . . . . . . . . . . . . . . . . . . . . . . . . . . . . . . . . . . . . . . . . . . . . . . . .

. . . . . . . . . . . . . . . . . . . . . . . . . . . . . . . . . . . . . . . . . . . . . . . . . . . . . . . . . . . . . . . . . . . . . . . . . . . .

## *Prayer for Today*

Dear Lord, help me remember what a difference it makes when I make time with You a priority in my morning. Awaken me in body and spirit each day with a desire to meet with You and to hear You speak words of affirmation, assurance and wisdom over my heart as I prepare to go into my day. In Jesus' name, Amen.

# DAY 53
## Winner's Circle

The LORD said to my Lord, "Sit in the place of honor at my right hand until I humble your enemies, making them a footstool under your feet." The LORD will extend your powerful kingdom from Jerusalem; you will rule over your enemies.

**– PSALMS 110:1-2 NLT**

I love football. I mean I really love college football. Especially when the Oklahoma Sooners are winning. The University of Oklahoma is my alma mater, so I feel as if I have special claim to them as my team. I love being part of a winning team. Do you feel that way too? I hope so. Let's keep this short and sweet. Don't be a loser, choose Christ. Christ wins. He wins everything. He is the Son of God, heir to all. "But in these last days he has spoken to us by his Son, whom he appointed the heir of all things, through whom also he created the world" as referenced in Hebrews 1:2 NLT

And to him was given dominion and glory and a kingdom, that all peoples, nations, and languages should serve him; his dominion is an everlasting dominion, which shall not pass away, and His kingdom one that shall not be destroyed. Yes, He is that good. The perfect champion. Jesus won when He completed His mission on the cross (although it looked like defeat until the perfectly timed resurrection comeback). The forever reigning champion has been declared and it is Jesus Christ. Yet, God decides when time is up for this game. When He blows the whistle (okay it's a trumpet) He then sends his Son to gather his team for a victory celebration.

What you do on this field called Earth matters for eternity. The final championship game will pass and another will come next year and the year after. God willing. But you only get one soul to surrender to the one you want to play for. Choose the winning team.

Duh, right? Sounds obvious. Choose to win, don't choose to lose. Believe it or not, a lot of people choose to lose. Remember, "the gate is wide and the way is easy that leads to destruction, and those who enter by it are many." Matthew 7:13 NLT Don't blow by this. I pray you think long and hard on whom you are playing for as you look toward a new year. If Christ has already made you part of His victorious team, good, but don't relax. Start playing like you mean it. This really isn't just a game after all (you do know this right?) Decide to work harder than ever in the upcoming months. The work of God always starts in the Word of God. Read it. If you feel like you may be on the losing side, then cry out to God for mercy. Ask Him to choose you to be His. Being won by God always starts with the Word of God.

*Day*

# 53

· · · · · · · · · · · · · · · · · · · · · · · · · · · · · · · · · · · · · · · · · · · · · · · · · · · · ·

· · · · · · · · · · · · · · · · · · · · · · · · · · · · · · · · · · · · · · · · · · · · · · · · · · · · ·

· · · · · · · · · · · · · · · · · · · · · · · · · · · · · · · · · · · · · · · · · · · · · · · · · · · · ·

· · · · · · · · · · · · · · · · · · · · · · · · · · · · · · · · · · · · · · · · · · · · · · · · · · · · ·

· · · · · · · · · · · · · · · · · · · · · · · · · · · · · · · · · · · · · · · · · · · · · · · · · · · · ·

· · · · · · · · · · · · · · · · · · · · · · · · · · · · · · · · · · · · · · · · · · · · · · · · · · · · ·

· · · · · · · · · · · · · · · · · · · · · · · · · · · · · · · · · · · · · · · · · · · · · · · · · · · · ·

## *Prayer for Today*

Dear God, cleanse me from anything that is blocking me from walking in victory. Fill me with peace and joy. Renew my strength so that I can soar like an eagle. May I run and not grow weary, may I walk in Your ways and not fall. Help me to handle the challenges of life with boldness because I am more than a conqueror through Christ Jesus. Keep my lamp burning and turn my darkness into light. Lord, Your ways are perfect, and Your word is flawless. I love and adore You. In Jesus' name, I believe and pray, Amen.

# DAY 54
## Adjust Your Focus

You will keep in perfect peace those whose minds are steadfast, because they trust in you.
**– ISAIAH 26:3 NIV**

What are you focusing on today? Are you focusing on your situation, or on God's promises? You may have all kinds of problems coming at you. Maybe you're feeling discouraged as new problems and challenges have popped up in your life. I have an iPhone and there is a new setting that allows you to take pictures in portrait mode. This feature allows you to focus on the object of interest and somewhat blur the other surrounding areas. When someone asks what they should do to ensure the power of God continues to work in their lives for unending peace and prosperity, I give them a simple answer: focus your mind on the Lord the same way you focus your camera lens on an object to get a clear image. When your mind (thoughts, emotions, and attention) is focused on God's Word, you're guaranteed to always walk in peace and prosperity. Your mind is a powerful tool given to you by God for transforming your life from glory to glory. If you'd give the right attention to the word of God, it doesn't matter the storms that come against you, you'll be at rest because the Lord Himself keeps you in "perfect peace." The Hebrew word for "peace" in Isaiah 26:3 is "shalom," which describes the "rest" of God, wherein is prosperity, health, strength, and salvation. This means that you can be as prosperous, successful and healthy as you want to be if you yield your mind to God's Word. But if we lose our focus, we are susceptible to the darkness. If you're currently walking in spiritual darkness, I encourage you to shift your focus. Focus your eyes on Jesus and His glory. The Word of God is your secret to a miraculous and supernatural life. So keep your focus on God's Word and divine peace and prosperity will be your continuous experience. Don't let it get you down. Don't let it take your focus off of God.

. . . . . . . . . . . . . . . . . . . . . . . . . . . . . . . . . . . . . . . . . . . . .

. . . . . . . . . . . . . . . . . . . . . . . . . . . . . . . . . . . . . . . . . . . . .

. . . . . . . . . . . . . . . . . . . . . . . . . . . . . . . . . . . . . . . . . . . . .

. . . . . . . . . . . . . . . . . . . . . . . . . . . . . . . . . . . . . . . . . . . . .

. . . . . . . . . . . . . . . . . . . . . . . . . . . . . . . . . . . . . . . . . . . . .

. . . . . . . . . . . . . . . . . . . . . . . . . . . . . . . . . . . . . . . . . . . . .

. . . . . . . . . . . . . . . . . . . . . . . . . . . . . . . . . . . . . . . . . . . . .

## Prayer for Today

Jesus, thank You for bringing light into my spiritual darkness. I confess that sometimes I focus on the things of this world rather than setting my sights on You. Help me to shift my focus. I want to look upon Your glory and have it transform me. In Your name I pray, Amen.

# DAY 55
## Living Your Best Life

I have been crucified with Christ and I no longer live, but Christ lives in me. The life I now live in the body, I live by faith in the Son of God, who loved me and gave himself for me.
### — GALATIANS 2:20 NIV

You don't have to retire from all those years of labor to begin living your best life. Many of us have visions of a better tomorrow, a future where we will exercise more, or find a career that we actually love, make more money, have more free time and so forth. If you're reading this, it is because you want more and you suspect you're capable of more. You have hopes and dreams and you're ready to create the life you want. Jesus lived and died to give us this gift of abundant life. So how do we go about receiving it? We see the need to change direction in our lives, the need for forgiveness for past sins, and the need to start down the path of discipleship with Jesus. But that is only the beginning. The next part is the "following" part, the "imitating Jesus" part. We begin to realize that there is left in our life a root of sin, from time to time we act unchristian, and we know that there must be more that God has for us than what we have. So what actually is our best life and how do we live it?

The most important word in the phrase "Living your best life" is "your." Strip away the Instagram filters and look at your own values objectively and with honesty. Figure out what's most important to you, what matters on an achievable level and go from there. What do you need to do to be satisfied with your life? Once you've figured that out, set some goals. Hate your busy city life? Then make time on the weekends to escape to the country. You're not energized by your career? Well, do something about it. Take tiny steps to inject things you like into your workplace, set new goals, talk to your boss about new responsibilities, or look for something new. Take a class, learn a skill, take up a new sport or hobby — everything is within your control. Ask God to take a certain habit away, to prune away a particular behavior and as God takes away those undesirable traits in your life, ask Him to fill those now-empty spaces with His love, His "likeness," and His presence. It is then that we find ourselves living out loud the best versions of ourselves. I believe we should be living life to its fullest, which is the life God intended for each of us to have and the life for which Jesus died. There is no reason to ever be ashamed of where you are in life. Not when you're doing your best. Not when you're in your best moment. There's always gonna be people to tell you "No." Or "You can't." Or "you shouldn't." Or even that it's just not in your cards. No matter what anybody says, you have to have the mindset that saids, "They may not see my potential but I'm still doing this and I will give it my best." Defy the odds. Take chances, take risks, try to appreciate the things you do have and surround yourself with people who bring out the best in you. Sometimes our happiest moments are among the most mundane made special by those they're shared with. Don't hinge your happiness on things you think will impress others — that's not living your best life. That's only living someone else's idea of it. This is the life that you can claim today. Why not you?

· · · · · · · · · · · · · · · · · · · · · · · · · · · · · · · · · · · · · · · · · · · · · · · · · · · · · ·

· · · · · · · · · · · · · · · · · · · · · · · · · · · · · · · · · · · · · · · · · · · · · · · · · · · · · ·

· · · · · · · · · · · · · · · · · · · · · · · · · · · · · · · · · · · · · · · · · · · · · · · · · · · · · ·

· · · · · · · · · · · · · · · · · · · · · · · · · · · · · · · · · · · · · · · · · · · · · · · · · · · · · ·

· · · · · · · · · · · · · · · · · · · · · · · · · · · · · · · · · · · · · · · · · · · · · · · · · · · · · ·

· · · · · · · · · · · · · · · · · · · · · · · · · · · · · · · · · · · · · · · · · · · · · · · · · · · · · ·

· · · · · · · · · · · · · · · · · · · · · · · · · · · · · · · · · · · · · · · · · · · · · · · · · · · · · ·

### Prayer for Today

God, help me love the life I live right now. Show me the good things I often overlook and help me be content with what I have. Forgive me when I compare myself to others, forgive me for longing for things outside of You and Your kingdom. Thank You for loving me right where I am, right as I am. Help me keep my eyes on You. In Jesus' name, Amen.

# DAY 56

## 3:00 A.M

Search me, O God, and know my heart; test me and know my anxious thoughts. Point out anything in me that offends you, and lead me along the path of everlasting life.

**– PSALMS 139:23-24 NLT**

It all began when my daughters moved out of the house several years ago to start a life on their own. To really sum it up, they did not like our respective household boundaries. The girls were barely in their twenties. My husband and I drew a line in the sand about certain conduct in our home we would not tolerate and they decided that was something they didn't want to conform to so they moved out to a high-rise apartment in the big city. All of this happened on the cusp of a major pandemic yet they still wanted to explore the world without restrictions or parental input. My stress levels peaked every time they pushed a new boundary and my anxiety was an all-time high when they moved out. The worry and anxiety level of a mother is hard to explain unless you are one. I didn't realize that I suffered through spells of insomnia until I started to journal my patterns. It seemed that every time I began to worry about their goings and comings, I would abruptly wake up at exactly 3:00 a.m. My anxiety always seemed to be worse at night. Although I would be dead tired, my brain would instantly move into an active state. A simple noise upstairs, a distant light in the house coming on or stray thoughts about something that happened in my day would send my mind racing down a rabbit hole of intrusive thoughts. Anxiety often convinces us that we have more power over our circumstances than we really do. Unfortunately, there are very few things that we can actually control: our actions, reactions, and choices. For example, we can decide what we serve for dinner, but we can't force anyone else to eat it. Life is going to happen whether you're afraid or not. It's very likely that most of the things you're worried about are not going to happen anyway but if they do, you're not alone, there is a guidance counselor available 24 hours a day, 7 days a week at no cost called the Holy Spirit who is equipped to comfort you in your time of need. I finally had to come to the realization that worrying accomplishes nothing other than wasting time. Whether it is a wayward child, a faithless spouse or an unpredictable supervisor. Whatever the "devil" you struggle with or in battle with, know that you don't have to do this alone. The enemy recognizes that God is your power-base. Therefore, his goal is to come between you and God. The enemy wants you to worry and get you distracted to help you forget that he was already defeated on the cross. You will never win a spiritual battle in your own strength. You will only be successful when you draw your strength from the power base, God himself. It will be there, where you will find the strength and the stamina you need to stand against satan and his tricks. Now, get some rest Beloved.

. . . . . . . . . . . . . . . . . . . . . . . . . . . . . . . . . . . . . . . . . . . . . . . . . . . . . . . .

. . . . . . . . . . . . . . . . . . . . . . . . . . . . . . . . . . . . . . . . . . . . . . . . . . . . . . . .

. . . . . . . . . . . . . . . . . . . . . . . . . . . . . . . . . . . . . . . . . . . . . . . . . . . . . . . .

. . . . . . . . . . . . . . . . . . . . . . . . . . . . . . . . . . . . . . . . . . . . . . . . . . . . . . . .

. . . . . . . . . . . . . . . . . . . . . . . . . . . . . . . . . . . . . . . . . . . . . . . . . . . . . . . .

. . . . . . . . . . . . . . . . . . . . . . . . . . . . . . . . . . . . . . . . . . . . . . . . . . . . . . . .

## *Prayer for Today*

Dear Jesus, I often feel alone. I feel like I'm the only one who is so messed up. But You assure me that's not true. Even when I don't feel You, You told me in Your Word that You're with me, that You understand. You know how I feel. Not just intellectually, but You feel it. Help me truly believe that. In Jesus' name, Amen.

# DAY 57
## Divine Interruptions

When Jesus heard him, he stopped and ordered that the man be brought to him.
As the man came near, Jesus asked him, "What do you want me to do for you?"
"Lord," he said, "I want to see!"
**— LUKE 18: 40-41 NLT**

Divine interruptions! Experts say that everyone experiences an alarming amount of time consumed each day by interruptions. Whether at work or at home, a phone call or an unexpected visit can easily deflect us from what we feel is our main purpose.

Not many of us like disruptions in our daily lives, especially when they cause inconvenience or a change of plans. But Jesus treated what appeared to be interruptions in a far different way. Time after time in the Gospels, we see the Lord stop what He is doing to help a person in need. While Jesus was on His way to Jerusalem where He would be crucified, a blind man begging by the side of the road called out, "Jesus, Son of David, have mercy on me!" (Luke 18:35–38). Some in the crowd told him to be quiet, but he kept calling out to Jesus. Jesus stopped and asked the man, "'What do you want me to do for you?' 'Lord, I want to see,' he replied. Jesus said to him, 'Receive your sight; your faith has healed you'" (vv. 41–42).

When our plans are interrupted by someone who genuinely needs help, we can ask the Lord for wisdom in how to respond with compassion. What we call an interruption may be a divine appointment the Lord has scheduled for that day. God may close a door because you're believing too small. If He opens the door, He is creating new possibilities that He wants to do in your life. An interruption may come because it's not the right time, or there are other people involved and they're not ready yet. Every delay doesn't mean you're not where you're supposed to be. God sees the big picture for your life. God knows where every road is leading. He knows the dead ends and shortcuts. Sometimes God will allow us to be inconvenienced so we can help someone else in need. We have to be willing to press through difficulty so we can be at the right place at the right time. The next time you're interrupted, delayed or inconvenienced, don't start thinking, "This is a pain. This is getting me off schedule." No, get a new perspective. Look for what God wants to do because it could be a divine interruption or divine protection. Trust Him today because He is directing your steps. Know that every disappointment, every delay, every interruption is orchestrated by the Most High God all for your good. God's delays are deliberate. He is in complete control and He promises that all things are going to work together for your good.

. . . . . . . . . . . . . . . . . . . . . . . . . . . . . . . . . . . . . . . . . . . . . . . . . . . . . . . . . . . . . . .

. . . . . . . . . . . . . . . . . . . . . . . . . . . . . . . . . . . . . . . . . . . . . . . . . . . . . . . . . . . . . . .

. . . . . . . . . . . . . . . . . . . . . . . . . . . . . . . . . . . . . . . . . . . . . . . . . . . . . . . . . . . . . . .

. . . . . . . . . . . . . . . . . . . . . . . . . . . . . . . . . . . . . . . . . . . . . . . . . . . . . . . . . . . . . . .

. . . . . . . . . . . . . . . . . . . . . . . . . . . . . . . . . . . . . . . . . . . . . . . . . . . . . . . . . . . . . . .

. . . . . . . . . . . . . . . . . . . . . . . . . . . . . . . . . . . . . . . . . . . . . . . . . . . . . . . . . . . . . . .

. . . . . . . . . . . . . . . . . . . . . . . . . . . . . . . . . . . . . . . . . . . . . . . . . . . . . . . . . . . . . . .

## Prayer for Today

All-powerful Father, I need Your presence right now. Please, step in with your divine power and assist me right now. Please show your glory and intercede for me! Bring Your saving grace and save me without hesitation. Show me the evil against me that You have under control. Please, come now to save me, O Lord! I pray in Jesus' name. Amen.

# Nothing Gets Better Than This

May he equip you with all you need for doing his will. May he produce in you, through the power of Jesus Christ, every good thing that is pleasing to him.

All glory to him forever and ever! Amen.

**– HEBREWS 13:21 NLT**

Do you ever limit God? Have you discounted certain dreams or ideas because you weren't skilled or qualified to do what was in your heart? There have been many times in my life where I have felt ill-equipped to accomplish what God has asked me to do. Where He was leading me was beyond my skill set, too uncomfortable and it put me in a position of vulnerability. No one likes to be vulnerable, right? Yet that's what it takes to follow Jesus sometimes. Being open to the uncomfortable, stepping out blindly, relying on His strength and not our own to perform the tasks ahead. When we decide to fully surrender, that's where our insecurity ends and His power begins.

The truth is, God equips the called, He doesn't call the equipped. And when He equips the called, He surrounds them with people who can help them through. That's what He did for me. He used people in my life to encourage me that I could do it, when I didn't think I could. He reassured me. He's bigger than I think. When I feel like I can't, He says, "You can't but I can."

Are you holding back on a dream because you feel inadequate? Are you resisting God's call to step out because you're not sure what to expect? Let me remind you that God has already laid the groundwork for you. He's gathered your helpers, planned the opportunities and He knows the end from the beginning. There's no place He's called you to that He hasn't already been. Your job is to trust Him. Know that He is bigger and greater than you can ever imagine. God's got you!

. . . . . . . . . . . . . . . . . . . . . . . . . . . . . . . . . . . . . . . . . . . . . . . . . . . . . . . . . . . . . . . . . . .

. . . . . . . . . . . . . . . . . . . . . . . . . . . . . . . . . . . . . . . . . . . . . . . . . . . . . . . . . . . . . . . . . . .

. . . . . . . . . . . . . . . . . . . . . . . . . . . . . . . . . . . . . . . . . . . . . . . . . . . . . . . . . . . . . . . . . . .

. . . . . . . . . . . . . . . . . . . . . . . . . . . . . . . . . . . . . . . . . . . . . . . . . . . . . . . . . . . . . . . . . . .

. . . . . . . . . . . . . . . . . . . . . . . . . . . . . . . . . . . . . . . . . . . . . . . . . . . . . . . . . . . . . . . . . . .

. . . . . . . . . . . . . . . . . . . . . . . . . . . . . . . . . . . . . . . . . . . . . . . . . . . . . . . . . . . . . . . . . . .

. . . . . . . . . . . . . . . . . . . . . . . . . . . . . . . . . . . . . . . . . . . . . . . . . . . . . . . . . . . . . . . . . . .

## Prayer for Today

Dear God, please give me strength when I am weak, love when I feel forsaken, courage when I am afraid, wisdom when I feel foolish, comfort when I am alone, hope when I feel rejected and peace when I am in turmoil. In Jesus' name, Amen.

Be alert and of a sober mind.
Your enemy the devil prowls around like a roaring lion looking for someone to devour. Resist him, standing firm in the faith, because you know that the family of believers throughout the world is undergoing the same kind of suffering.
**— 1 PETER 5:8-9 NIV**

I call her my inner voice or my hater. Suzy, she is always saying things that are counterproductive and contradictory to who God tells me I am. The enemy will use whatever it takes to make us believe his lies. It's to his benefit to convince you that you are behind, not good enough, not pretty enough or capable of doing the very thing God has called you to do. The enemy reminds us of our limitations in an effort to steal our joy and weaken our faith. As long as we continue to listen to the lies, we will allow the enemy's voice to ring louder than God's word. The enemy will twist words to make them sound like the truth in an effort to cater to his plan. So we have to choose to believe what God has said about us over what the enemy says. I don't know who your inner voice is or if you have a name for her but there comes a time you need to put her in check and remind her that she does not have dominion over your life, your mind or your body! You might be surprised at the people around you who secretly hate themselves. Oftentimes it's people you look up to and love. Hating yourself doesn't make you a bad person or unworthy of love. But many of the times the person they dislike is their negative, self-sabotaging and self-doubting voice.

We all have two voices inside us. There's the one that is nurturing and uplifting—the voice that empowers us to lean into what we love, the voice that speaks the language of confidence, encouragement, and possibility. That's the voice of the Holy Spirit. Then there's the one that is critical and discouraging—the voice that weighs us down like gravity, rendering us incapable of growing into who we ought to become. That second voice is who I call "Sabotaging Sally." No she doesn't talk to me, that would be an issue but it's my inner critic who is always creating doubt to hold me back from seeing the change I want to create in my life and what God has created for me. The Bible outlines very clearly that there is an enemy to God and there's an enemy to us. And his desire is to kill, steal and destroy. One of the main ways he attempts to destroy us is through mind games. In John 8, it talks about the enemy and Jesus actually describes him and says he is the father of lies—that when he speaks, he speaks lies. So don't believe the hype of the enemy because he is an enemy of the state, or better yet the state of mind.

· · · · · · · · · · · · · · · · · · · · · · · · · · · · · · · · · · · · · · · · · · · · · · · · · · · · · · ·

· · · · · · · · · · · · · · · · · · · · · · · · · · · · · · · · · · · · · · · · · · · · · · · · · · · · · · ·

· · · · · · · · · · · · · · · · · · · · · · · · · · · · · · · · · · · · · · · · · · · · · · · · · · · · · · ·

· · · · · · · · · · · · · · · · · · · · · · · · · · · · · · · · · · · · · · · · · · · · · · · · · · · · · · ·

· · · · · · · · · · · · · · · · · · · · · · · · · · · · · · · · · · · · · · · · · · · · · · · · · · · · · · ·

· · · · · · · · · · · · · · · · · · · · · · · · · · · · · · · · · · · · · · · · · · · · · · · · · · · · · · ·

· · · · · · · · · · · · · · · · · · · · · · · · · · · · · · · · · · · · · · · · · · · · · · · · · · · · · · ·

## *Prayer for Today*

Abba Father, I declare that today is MY DAY! I choose to stand against the attacks of the enemy! He will not have further control over me. I also declare that I will renew my mind with the things of you, as the battle has already been won. My confession is that, by the FINISHED work of Jesus, I can claim VICTORY over my life. I have the peace of mind and the assurance that the Holy Spirit continues to dwell in me and grants me peace. In the name of Jesus, I renounce those thoughts that hold my mind captive. These things I declare in Jesus' Name, AMEN!

# DAY 60
## Dare to Dream

Joseph had a dream and when he told it to his brothers, they hated him all the more.
**– GENESIS 37:5 NIV**

As we mature in life, our dreams take the back seat due to many circumstances that life throws our way. Dreams are given by God and as a believer, a specific dream was deposited into each of us to fulfill on the earth. I think one of the best things we can do to make our everyday lives better is to dream big, bold, faith-filled dreams. You can dream about what the future holds, about what new things you can accomplish with God's help. Keeping in mind that God's Word says that He can do much more than we could ever imagine or dream (see Ephesians 3:20). However, in order to realize any dream—a new career, a stronger marriage, big things for your children—it's important to look at and adjust your attitude. When you change your attitude from pessimism to optimism, from fear to faith, you are on the road to seeing your dreams come true. For example, when you're tempted to think, "it's too hard or, I'm too old," remind yourself that your attitude determines your altitude. Are you looking in a mirror or gazing through a window? Let's think about this for a minute. When you look at a mirror, you only are able to see one possibility and one dream. But when you look through a window, you can see all of the opportunities that are waiting for you. Windows can provide light, clarity, hope, new expectations and can give you a glimpse of what is to come. Don't stop believing and dreaming, girl!

. . . . . . . . . . . . . . . . . . . . . . . . . . . . . . . . . . . . . . . . . . . . . . . . . . . . . . . . . . . . . . . .

. . . . . . . . . . . . . . . . . . . . . . . . . . . . . . . . . . . . . . . . . . . . . . . . . . . . . . . . . . . . . . . .

. . . . . . . . . . . . . . . . . . . . . . . . . . . . . . . . . . . . . . . . . . . . . . . . . . . . . . . . . . . . . . . .

. . . . . . . . . . . . . . . . . . . . . . . . . . . . . . . . . . . . . . . . . . . . . . . . . . . . . . . . . . . . . . . .

. . . . . . . . . . . . . . . . . . . . . . . . . . . . . . . . . . . . . . . . . . . . . . . . . . . . . . . . . . . . . . . .

. . . . . . . . . . . . . . . . . . . . . . . . . . . . . . . . . . . . . . . . . . . . . . . . . . . . . . . . . . . . . . . .

. . . . . . . . . . . . . . . . . . . . . . . . . . . . . . . . . . . . . . . . . . . . . . . . . . . . . . . . . . . . . . . .

## Prayer for Today

Dear Lord, thank You for the ability to dream. Help me to dream and to pursue the dreams You have given me. Help me have faith and trust in You daily. Thank You for Your unfailing and unconditional love. In Jesus' Name, Amen.

# DAY 61
## Talitha Koum

Holding her hand, he said to her, "Talitha koum," which means "Little girl, get up!" And the girl, who was twelve years old, immediately stood up and walked around! They were overwhelmed and totally amazed.

**— MARK 5:41-42 NLT**

Are you weak? Stressed? Battling depression? Do you need more energy to run this race of life that you're in? Is your strength depleted? God can help. Fortunately, our Creator gives us many scriptures that relate to how we can have strength in Him. It doesn't matter what other people say. Did you know that there is greatness within you. God designed you to reach your full potential. To be powerful beyond measure. To have success and joy and abundance in your life. Don't let fear make you quit. Don't let the terror of what "could" happen affect how you take the next step forward.

Girl, get up! You've been given the incredible gift of God's peace. This means you don't have to let fear trouble your heart. You don't have to let the unknown shake you to the core. It doesn't matter how dead you were before God stepped in because now He wants you to take action and get back up again! Last year, last week, even what you did last night does not define you. Your sin, your shame, your accolades, your community and your family name – none of them matter. The fruit produced after God intervenes is everlasting and ever changing because when He steps into your situation or circumstance He renews, revitalizes, restores and rejuvenates you back to His factory settings. You are everything you are because He brought you back. You are everything you are because you are loved. You are everything you are because you've been made alive again. Nothing in your life is beyond resurrection and nothing in your life is too dead for His healing touch to fix it. Believe me sister in Christ, now is the time to get up because you can do everything God designed you to do.

. . . . . . . . . . . . . . . . . . . . . . . . . . . . . . . . . . . . . . . . . . . . .

. . . . . . . . . . . . . . . . . . . . . . . . . . . . . . . . . . . . . . . . . . . . .

. . . . . . . . . . . . . . . . . . . . . . . . . . . . . . . . . . . . . . . . . . . . .

. . . . . . . . . . . . . . . . . . . . . . . . . . . . . . . . . . . . . . . . . . . . .

. . . . . . . . . . . . . . . . . . . . . . . . . . . . . . . . . . . . . . . . . . . . .

. . . . . . . . . . . . . . . . . . . . . . . . . . . . . . . . . . . . . . . . . . . . .

. . . . . . . . . . . . . . . . . . . . . . . . . . . . . . . . . . . . . . . . . . . . .

## *Prayer for Today*

Dear Heavenly Father, Your ways are higher than my ways. I pray for power and strength to surrender my way and follow Your best way. I trust You Lord.

In Jesus' name, Amen.

# DAY 62
## Ready to Forgive

Do not take revenge, my dear friends, but leave room for God's wrath, for it is written: "It is mine to avenge; I will repay, says the Lord.
**— ROMANS 12:19 NIV**

I hate to bring up this word, but I don't have a choice. It's the last word any of us wants to hear echoing back and forth in a pit we've been thrown into. You already know what this word is, and you're probably sick of hearing it. But we have to hear that difficult word again: forgive. It's a tough thing to do, but we've got to forgive, especially — those who don't care to be forgiven. I know what you're thinking, if you knew what happened to me, you wouldn't be able to forgive them either. You think you can't forgive? I felt the same way. I heard over and over how I had to forgive, because the Lord forgave me. That is easily said but not easily done. You see, I started out in a pit of innocence, but through the years my bitterness rearranged the furniture until it was nothing more than a well-camouflaged pit of sin. But I thought forgiving my pit-throwers would make what happened all right. But, to my surprise, it didn't. And still hasn't. What I didn't understand about forgiveness was that it would make "me" all right. One day I finally began getting that message and I'm praying right now that this is that day for you. Like all of God's commands, His call to forgive is for your good. Forgiveness is a process and that process leads to freedom. Your freedom. Forgiveness is not an emotion; it is a decision. Forgiveness is to intentionally end that period in our lives that caused us pain. Forgiveness allows us to remove the power from the situation or person that may have hurt us. It is the act of leaving pain at a specific place so that you may never feel it again. Focusing on what is broken will never set you free, and when you're not free you can't be released. It is time to loosen your grip on the unforgiveness, bitterness, resentment, hatred and anger that is keeping you from experiencing the fullness of God. Unforgiveness is an instant way to block your blessing that may be on its way.

. . . . . . . . . . . . . . . . . . . . . . . . . . . . . . . . . . . . . . . . . . . . . . . . . . . . . . . . . . . . . . . . . . . . . .

. . . . . . . . . . . . . . . . . . . . . . . . . . . . . . . . . . . . . . . . . . . . . . . . . . . . . . . . . . . . . . . . . . . . . .

. . . . . . . . . . . . . . . . . . . . . . . . . . . . . . . . . . . . . . . . . . . . . . . . . . . . . . . . . . . . . . . . . . . . . .

. . . . . . . . . . . . . . . . . . . . . . . . . . . . . . . . . . . . . . . . . . . . . . . . . . . . . . . . . . . . . . . . . . . . . .

. . . . . . . . . . . . . . . . . . . . . . . . . . . . . . . . . . . . . . . . . . . . . . . . . . . . . . . . . . . . . . . . . . . . . .

. . . . . . . . . . . . . . . . . . . . . . . . . . . . . . . . . . . . . . . . . . . . . . . . . . . . . . . . . . . . . . . . . . . . . .

. . . . . . . . . . . . . . . . . . . . . . . . . . . . . . . . . . . . . . . . . . . . . . . . . . . . . . . . . . . . . . . . . . . . . .

## Prayer for Today

Dear Lord, I thank You for the power of forgiveness and I choose to forgive everyone who has hurt me. Help me set [name anyone who has offended you] free and release them to You (Romans 12:19). Help me bless those who have hurt me (Romans 12:14). Help me walk in righteousness, peace, and joy, demonstrating Your life here on earth. I choose to be kind and compassionate, forgiving others, just as You forgave me. In Jesus' name, Amen.

# Be A Blessing

*So encourage each other and build each other up, just as you are already doing.*
**– 1 THESSALONIANS 5:11 NLT**

What are you doing to help someone else? Believe it or not, being intentional to make a difference in others' lives is evidence of your love for God. The cycle of love that pours into your life is not complete until it's pouring out of you to meet other people's needs. If love has no action to back it up, then it becomes empty words with no power. God proved His love for us by giving His only Son to die for our sins, and we can prove our love for Him by letting Him work through us to feed His sheep—to help hurting people.

An African proverb says, "There is only one crime worse than murder on the desert, and that is to know where the water is and not tell anyone else." God has led us to Christ, the living water. He has blessed us with His salvation and He promises to bless us even more abundantly in the future. But He didn't save us so that we could sit in the lifeboat feeling warm and cozy, oblivious to the lost souls in the world. He saved us so that we may become a blessing to others. If you're saved but you don't have your focus on blessing others, you've only got half the picture. He blessed you so that you may be a blessing. Don't wait to feel like being a blessing—start doing it on purpose. Maybe you have an elderly neighbor who needs help taking care of their yard. Maybe you have a friend who's going through a tough time right now and would love to hear from you. Or maybe you know a single mom who could really use a helping hand. Whoever it is, I guarantee you there's someone in your path that you can bless today, even if it's in a seemingly small way. As you take steps to make their day better, it will add joy to your life. The truth is, it is God's will for you to connect with people and to use your life to reveal His love to those around you. But for that to happen, you have to be willing to stop, take time, open up your heart and share your life with them. And that, my friend, takes faith!

*Day*

# 63

. . . . . . . . . . . . . . . . . . . . . . . . . . . . . . . . . . . . . . . . . . . . . . . . . . . . . . . . . . . . . . . . . . . . . . .

. . . . . . . . . . . . . . . . . . . . . . . . . . . . . . . . . . . . . . . . . . . . . . . . . . . . . . . . . . . . . . . . . . . . . . .

. . . . . . . . . . . . . . . . . . . . . . . . . . . . . . . . . . . . . . . . . . . . . . . . . . . . . . . . . . . . . . . . . . . . . . .

. . . . . . . . . . . . . . . . . . . . . . . . . . . . . . . . . . . . . . . . . . . . . . . . . . . . . . . . . . . . . . . . . . . . . . .

. . . . . . . . . . . . . . . . . . . . . . . . . . . . . . . . . . . . . . . . . . . . . . . . . . . . . . . . . . . . . . . . . . . . . . .

. . . . . . . . . . . . . . . . . . . . . . . . . . . . . . . . . . . . . . . . . . . . . . . . . . . . . . . . . . . . . . . . . . . . . . .

. . . . . . . . . . . . . . . . . . . . . . . . . . . . . . . . . . . . . . . . . . . . . . . . . . . . . . . . . . . . . . . . . . . . . . .

## Prayer for Today

Heavenly Father, please show me who You want me to be kind to today and how I can make someone's day better. Thank You for Your love and for helping me share Your love with other people around me today. In Jesus' name, Amen.

# DAY 64
## *You're So Worthy*

Do not let your hearts be troubled. You believe in God; believe also in me.
### – JOHN 14:1 NIV

When you finally believe you can have anything you want, you'll stop settling. Pause for just a second and take a deep breath. Now read the following statement and really take it in. "You are worthy of love." What happens inside when you read that statement? Does your heart open up and do you breathe a sigh of relief? Or do you cringe inside and immediately dismiss it? As the author Brene Brown once said," There is no prerequisite to worthiness." Has anyone told you that you're beautiful today? Well, you are. Has anyone told you that you're loved today? Well, you are. Has anyone told you that you're valuable today? Well, you are. You are worthy and perfectly you, you are loved far more than you could ever imagine and you are more valuable than any rare jewel or diamond. In the world today, it is so easy to forget who we are and what we deserve. In the routine of life, it's easy to decide to settle. When we don't understand our worth, consequently, we don't understand what we deserve. When we don't respect ourselves, how can we expect anyone else to respect us? A misinterpretation of who we are causes a ripple effect into every aspect of our lives. We have to learn who we are and what we deserve. We have to understand that the things we want from others, we first have to give to ourselves. We have to know our self-worth. Self-worth is a concept we often hear about, but something that we give little thought to. It's something we brush off and we miss the importance of it. But in reality, it's one of the most important things for us to understand. So allow me to get the record straight. You deserve respect. When we learn to respect ourselves, others begin to respect us too. When we walk with our heads held high and we're proud of the person we are, other people notice—because you're respect-able, you're valuable and you're one of a kind. So, why not be proud of that? Why not have the people around you respect that about you?

You deserve encouragement. So be an encourager to the people around you. We so often forget the impact of a simple compliment. We often think positive things about other people, whether it's "I like her outfit" or "She has awesome hair," but I challenge you to actually say those things out loud. See what happens when you begin to encourage those around you. It doesn't just help those around, but it helps you too! You deserve love. Love is something every single one of us deserves. Love isn't just for your neighbor who lives next door, the supermodel or just for the girl who seems to have it all together. It's for you and me as well. You are worthy of being loved. So show people that by first loving yourself. There's nothing more empowering than a girl who believes in herself, so believe that you deserve to be loved.

And lastly, you deserve to give oneself grace. When we learn our worth, and we learn to value ourselves and expect all these things, we learn that happiness isn't that hard to have. Don't rob yourself of the joy and the life that was planned for you. Stop being so hard on yourself and know that we are imperfect people living in an imperfect world, but also know that what you do with it is up to you. It's not about what circumstances are given to you, but how you handle them.

. . . . . . . . . . . . . . . . . . . . . . . . . . . . . . . . . . . . . . . . . . . . . . .

. . . . . . . . . . . . . . . . . . . . . . . . . . . . . . . . . . . . . . . . . . . . . . .

. . . . . . . . . . . . . . . . . . . . . . . . . . . . . . . . . . . . . . . . . . . . . . .

. . . . . . . . . . . . . . . . . . . . . . . . . . . . . . . . . . . . . . . . . . . . . . .

. . . . . . . . . . . . . . . . . . . . . . . . . . . . . . . . . . . . . . . . . . . . . . .

. . . . . . . . . . . . . . . . . . . . . . . . . . . . . . . . . . . . . . . . . . . . . . .

. . . . . . . . . . . . . . . . . . . . . . . . . . . . . . . . . . . . . . . . . . . . . . .

## Prayer for Today

Heavenly Father, I come to You today in need of healing and self-love. Not only the words and actions of others but my own negative thoughts and self-criticism stand against me. I humbly pray for Your grace and love to hold me and lift me beyond this pain. I know I am not perfect but I am Your child and worthy of love. Guide me, Lord God. Show me how to love myself as You love me. Help me to see myself through Your eyes. Fill me with Your light and Your peace. In Jesus' name, Amen.

# DAY 65
## When God, When?

And let us not grow weary in well doing: for in due season we shall reap, if we faint not.
**– GALATIANS 6:9 KJV**

Have you ever said, "When God, when?" And His response to you is "In due season." So many times I want things now! I want to see the fruit of my sowing now as I cry out to God, "I've been faithful to sow! I am your servant; hear my cries. When Lord? When will you come and heal? When will you increase my substance? When will you answer my prayers?" You've probably heard the phrase, "Good things come to those who wait." It is somewhat true. I'd like to add to that the words, "...on God while continuing to sow." If you continue to sow the seeds God has given you to sow, you will reap a good harvest in due season. However, only He knows when that season is. Your job is to keep watering and keep sowing precious seeds. God has perfect timing for everything in your life. Sometimes He answers prayers quickly. Other times He waits until He knows you are ready to use His gifts wisely. The wait is not always easy. Impatience, frustration, and disappointment can build because you're waiting for things to happen quickly. It is only when you learn to respect, appreciate and most of all, trust the times of waiting that God really goes to work behind the scenes in earnest. God hears you and He will answer your prayers. If you're willing to wait on His perfect timing, your dreams will be fulfilled with all the blessings of His love. So while you're waiting, cultivate your crops. Some seasons are short and some are long, but He knows your "due season" for a bountiful harvest. Don't stop sowing. Harvest time is coming!

Day

# 65

· · · · · · · · · · · · · · · · · · · · · · · · · · · · · · · · · · · · · · · · · · · · · · · · · · · · · · · · · · · · · · · · ·

· · · · · · · · · · · · · · · · · · · · · · · · · · · · · · · · · · · · · · · · · · · · · · · · · · · · · · · · · · · · · · · · ·

· · · · · · · · · · · · · · · · · · · · · · · · · · · · · · · · · · · · · · · · · · · · · · · · · · · · · · · · · · · · · · · · ·

· · · · · · · · · · · · · · · · · · · · · · · · · · · · · · · · · · · · · · · · · · · · · · · · · · · · · · · · · · · · · · · · ·

· · · · · · · · · · · · · · · · · · · · · · · · · · · · · · · · · · · · · · · · · · · · · · · · · · · · · · · · · · · · · · · · ·

· · · · · · · · · · · · · · · · · · · · · · · · · · · · · · · · · · · · · · · · · · · · · · · · · · · · · · · · · · · · · · · · ·

· · · · · · · · · · · · · · · · · · · · · · · · · · · · · · · · · · · · · · · · · · · · · · · · · · · · · · · · · · · · · · · · ·

## *Prayer for Today*

Father God and Lord of our harvest, give me the necessary strength for this current season of life. Help me become more patient and obedient so that I may reap a bountiful harvest in due season! In Jesus' mighty name, Amen.

# When God Calls, You Answer

But Jonah arose to flee to Tarshish from the presence of the Lord.
**– JONAH 1:3 NKJV**

The Holy Spirit is a gentleman. He doesn't knock down your door or snatch you out of bed to go forth and fulfill God's assignment for your life. No, He doesn't yell from the rooftops or bogard His way into your life. The Holy Spirit comes in a still quiet voice calling you in the midst of your jam-packed day or in the busyness of life when you seem to have it all together. Right when you've gotten settled into the dream job or career or when you've just solidified your role in the company or just at the moment when you're ready to embark on your bucket list journey. That's when God calls you to missions in another country or the inner city to proclaim the gospel to those in need of salvation. I don't know about you but there have been times when the call of God came at what I considered the most inconvenient time in my life. But through wisdom, I have learned a very valuable lesson. When God calls, you better answer! Just like Jonah, there have been moments when I heard the voice of God telling me to go somewhere but because I was too stubborn or just too self-centered, I ignored the call and it ended up being costly in the long run. But thank God for second chances. After looking back over my life and seeing how many blessings I missed out on because I didn't answer the call of God, I have finally come to the conclusion that there are certain things God has assigned me to do that are specifically for me and me alone to accomplish. Regardless of how afraid I am, regardless of how I don't understand how it will benefit me in the long run or no matter how I can't perceive how it will help others. The key is obedience. Once God knows He can rely on you and that you are a willing vessel, that's when He will open up the windows of heaven and pour out the blessings that you won't have room enough to receive.

· · · · · · · · · · · · · · · · · · · · · · · · · · · · · · · · · · · · · · · · · · · · · · · · · · · · · · · · · · · · · · · · · · · · · · · · · · · · ·

· · · · · · · · · · · · · · · · · · · · · · · · · · · · · · · · · · · · · · · · · · · · · · · · · · · · · · · · · · · · · · · · · · · · · · · · · · · · ·

· · · · · · · · · · · · · · · · · · · · · · · · · · · · · · · · · · · · · · · · · · · · · · · · · · · · · · · · · · · · · · · · · · · · · · · · · · · · ·

· · · · · · · · · · · · · · · · · · · · · · · · · · · · · · · · · · · · · · · · · · · · · · · · · · · · · · · · · · · · · · · · · · · · · · · · · · · · ·

· · · · · · · · · · · · · · · · · · · · · · · · · · · · · · · · · · · · · · · · · · · · · · · · · · · · · · · · · · · · · · · · · · · · · · · · · · · · ·

· · · · · · · · · · · · · · · · · · · · · · · · · · · · · · · · · · · · · · · · · · · · · · · · · · · · · · · · · · · · · · · · · · · · · · · · · · · · ·

· · · · · · · · · · · · · · · · · · · · · · · · · · · · · · · · · · · · · · · · · · · · · · · · · · · · · · · · · · · · · · · · · · · · · · · · · · · · ·

## *Prayer for Today*

Lord, I repent for being disobedient to Your calling on my life. I have been running in the opposite direction too long and I am tired of running from the assignment You've called me to fulfill. Forgive me and give me a new heart and a new chance to be who You've called me to be. Give me the power to do Your will and use me to be a light to those in darkness. In Jesus' name, Amen.

# DAY 67
## Miraculous God

Jesus looked at them and said, "With man this is impossible, but not with God; all things are possible with God."
**— MARK 10:27 NIV**

I love what David said in the Bible, "God, my times are in your hands." He was saying, "God, I don't know when it's going to happen, but I know You know what's best for me." So I'm going to go out today expecting good things. It is always good to stir up our faith and remember that God is a God of miracles. As the prophet Jeremiah said, nothing is too difficult for Him! Because we believe His Word, we can be confident that "with God all things are possible" (see Matt. 19:26). You may feel that your life is a mess right now and that nothing will ever change. For a believer, that's just not true. God can take your biggest mess and turn it into your biggest miracle. In our natural minds, there are certain things we think of as too difficult for us. You may be thinking about a situation right now that seems too hard for you. Maybe it's getting out of debt. Maybe it's losing weight and becoming physically fit. Maybe it's doing your part to see a breakthrough in your marriage or family. Whatever your circumstances are, if there is something that seems too difficult for you, I have good news today: It's not too hard for God. Let me remind you that in the Old Testament, God reached down from heaven and parted the Red Sea so His people could escape from their enemies and walk through it on dry land (see Exodus 14:21–22). If we were to visit the ocean, we would not be able to hold back even a handful of water, but God held back all of it. This miraculous deliverance positioned His people to finally enter into the great promises He had for them!

Think also about how hard you may have tried to change yourself or to change other people at times. That is very hard to do. But God can take hard, wounded, sinful, bitter hearts and make them soft, whole, strong, holy, loving, and forgiving. If He can do that, then I believe He can do anything. The salvation and transformation He does in us is truly miraculous. In the New Testament, Jesus did all kinds of miracles. Nothing was too difficult for Him—not turning five loaves and two fish into a meal that fed five thousand people (see Mark 6:41–44), not healing a woman who had been bleeding for twelve years (see Luke 8:43–48), not raising someone from the dead (see Luke 8:49–55), not even walking on water (see Matthew 14:22–25). All these things would definitely be too hard for us, but not for Him.

Today, I encourage you to spend some time thinking about the things you think are too hard for you. Take each one and surrender it to God. Release it and tell Him that you trust Him with it completely and that you believe nothing is too difficult for Him.

. . . . . . . . . . . . . . . . . . . . . . . . . . . . . . . . . . . . . . . . . . . . . .

. . . . . . . . . . . . . . . . . . . . . . . . . . . . . . . . . . . . . . . . . . . . . .

. . . . . . . . . . . . . . . . . . . . . . . . . . . . . . . . . . . . . . . . . . . . . .

. . . . . . . . . . . . . . . . . . . . . . . . . . . . . . . . . . . . . . . . . . . . . .

. . . . . . . . . . . . . . . . . . . . . . . . . . . . . . . . . . . . . . . . . . . . . .

. . . . . . . . . . . . . . . . . . . . . . . . . . . . . . . . . . . . . . . . . . . . . .

## Prayer for Today

Father God, I often find myself overwhelmed by circumstances that are beyond my control and I am easily distracted by things that don't matter. Please forgive me for not consistently placing my trust in You. Even when I am faced with intense situations, You are still with me. You are the Creator of peace and I can have access to Your peace-filled presence whenever I draw near to You. So instead of silencing Your Holy Spirit when I start to feel anxious or discouraged, help me to make room in my heart and mind to experience the peace You freely give. And even if it doesn't happen, I'm not going to go to bed disappointed. I'm going to go to bed knowing that I'm one day closer to seeing my dreams and desires come to pass! In Jesus' name, Amen.

# DAY 68
## Be Salty & Light

In the same way, let your light shine before others, that they may see your good deeds and glorify your Father in heaven.
**—MATTHEW 5:16 NIV**

Have you ever heard someone say, "There's just something about them?" People sometimes say this when they can't quite put their finger on what it is that makes a person stand out from the crowd. I like when I hear it said about someone who's a Christian. Because when we are led by the Holy Spirit and God's love flows through us, there is something that just draws attention—something beautiful and unique.

The Bible says that Christians are the salt of the earth and the light of the world. On the job, in the grocery store, even among unsaved friends and family members, God's people are there to bring seasoning to an unsavory situation. As Christians, we are the ones who can help others find what they need in a relationship with God. But, in Matthew 5, Jesus asks, "What good is it if salt loses its flavor?" It seems that somewhere along the way, the lines between godliness and ungodliness have gotten blurred. Things that would have been considered wrong 20 or 30 years ago seem to be "not so bad" today. I wonder what the next 20 years will bring if this ideology continues. We may need to ask ourselves: What are we showing the world? What is it that keeps us "salty?" How do we, as Christians, keep our light shining in the darkness around us? Aside from the cross necklaces and bumper stickers, what sets us apart in the world? I believe it's holiness. And when I say that, I don't mean religion. I'm not talking about a list of do's and don'ts or going to church on Sunday mornings just to do your Christian duty one day a week. Religious legalism only gives us rules to follow but no real help to follow them! When I say holiness, I'm talking about behavior that's borne out of a personal, intimate relationship with God. I'm talking about a place of consecration that causes us to be obedient to the Holy Spirit in our everyday lives...something that makes us walk in love toward others, looking for ways to be a blessing to them. I'm talking about what makes us authentically, uniquely and innately good, holy...real!

It's about being, rather than doing. That's something the world needs to see in us. It's not up to us to preach to everyone around us, telling them everything that's wrong with them. We are simply to be light in the darkness around us so they can find their way to Jesus. Don't worry if you feel like you haven't "arrived." The fact that you are dissatisfied with where you are or that you're seeking to be a better person means you are making progress. God didn't promise the process would be fast...or easy...or feel good all the time. Just be thankful for His love and grace while He works.

Now, at any point in the process, we can always be a blessing. I like to say we should bloom where we are planted. We can be good to people anytime. We just need to be real. To share our struggles as well as our victories. Wherever we are in our process of growing in holiness, it's important to remember the world is watching. And they need to see someone who may not be perfect, but "there's just something about them!" You are so much more valuable to everyone around you and to the world if you begin every day knowing exactly who you are and try to be the best, brightest version of yourself.

Be the salt. Be the light. And glorify your Father in heaven.

. . . . . . . . . . . . . . . . . . . . . . . . . . . . . . . . . . . . . . . . . . . . . . . . . . .

. . . . . . . . . . . . . . . . . . . . . . . . . . . . . . . . . . . . . . . . . . . . . . . . . . .

. . . . . . . . . . . . . . . . . . . . . . . . . . . . . . . . . . . . . . . . . . . . . . . . . . .

. . . . . . . . . . . . . . . . . . . . . . . . . . . . . . . . . . . . . . . . . . . . . . . . . . .

. . . . . . . . . . . . . . . . . . . . . . . . . . . . . . . . . . . . . . . . . . . . . . . . . . .

. . . . . . . . . . . . . . . . . . . . . . . . . . . . . . . . . . . . . . . . . . . . . . . . . . .

. . . . . . . . . . . . . . . . . . . . . . . . . . . . . . . . . . . . . . . . . . . . . . . . . . .

## Prayer for Today

Dear Lord, may I be Your light and salt in this world, Your representative of all that is good and hopeful. In Jesus' name, Amen.

# *Don't Settle*

Terah took his son Abram, his grandson Lot son of Haran, and his daughter-in-law Sarai, the wife of his son Abram, and together they set out from Ur of the Chaldeans to go to Canaan. But when they came to Harran, they settled there.

**— GENESIS 11:31 NIV**

People have a tendency to settle for mediocrity in many aspects of their lives on a daily basis. We accept jobs we hate, we deal with friends who let us down and we let our significant others get away with craziness. Why do people choose to be complacent instead of moving where there are better opportunities? Why do we choose to settle for less than God's best for our lives? If that means going through a tunnel of conflict, take the tunnel. In the middle of the tunnel, it will be dark, and you will want to run back to the light. But you've got to keep going until you come out on the other side into the light. Are you pressing 'on toward the goal to win the prize for which God has called [you]' (Philippians 3:14 NIV), or have you 'settled' along the way?

God made a pact with Abraham—one that continues to influence the modern world. A lesser-known fact is that years earlier Abraham's father, Terah, 'set out to go to Canaan,' the land of abundance where God later called Abraham. But Terah never made it. When they came to Haran, they settled there. No question, it couldn't have been easy traveling hundreds of miles across rough terrain with flocks, herds, children and servants. Can you imagine the sheer logistics? Remember, there were no professional movers to pack and load their stuff. Finally Terah decided they couldn't go any farther, so they settled where they were comfortable. I wonder how many times we've done the same thing? Settled. You have a big dream to excel in your career, as a parent and in our walk with God, but we give up and settle. We get started, but things get difficult and achieving our goal doesn't happen as quickly as we hoped. Perhaps similar to Abraham's father we say, "Let's just settle here. It's not really what we wanted, but it's good enough." Don't fall into that trap, sis. You were made for more than "good enough." Don't settle for a little love and joy, a bit of peace and contentment, or a small helping of happiness. Pull up stakes, pack your tents, get your belongings and start moving forward. Enlarge your vision. You may have experienced a delay or detour but you can begin again today. Don't allow complacency or fear to keep you from reaching your goals and potential. Get up and start moving forward, you have another destination to get to before it gets too dark. Journey with God, He will take you places you can't even imagine.

. . . . . . . . . . . . . . . . . . . . . . . . . . . . . . . . . . . . . . . . . . . . . . . . . . . . . . . . . . .

. . . . . . . . . . . . . . . . . . . . . . . . . . . . . . . . . . . . . . . . . . . . . . . . . . . . . . . . . . .

. . . . . . . . . . . . . . . . . . . . . . . . . . . . . . . . . . . . . . . . . . . . . . . . . . . . . . . . . . .

. . . . . . . . . . . . . . . . . . . . . . . . . . . . . . . . . . . . . . . . . . . . . . . . . . . . . . . . . . .

. . . . . . . . . . . . . . . . . . . . . . . . . . . . . . . . . . . . . . . . . . . . . . . . . . . . . . . . . . .

. . . . . . . . . . . . . . . . . . . . . . . . . . . . . . . . . . . . . . . . . . . . . . . . . . . . . . . . . . .

## *Prayer for Today*

Father, I thank You that this is the day that You have made and we will rejoice and be glad in it. I thank You that You have given us 365 days in which we have new opportunities to fulfill the plans You have for us. I thank You Lord, that You have predestined us in the way that we should go and You have personally planned in advance the work for each of us to do. I thank You that there are No "if's" in your plans for us. The only "if" in your plan for us is in obedience to do what You ask. I pray that You will help us to turn our "if's" into "when's" for You are a faithful God and there should never be an "if" before our prayers. Help us to never waiver in our faith but to be confident that when we pray You always hear us and You always answer. Help us to rid ourselves of the doubting "if's" and know that it gives You good pleasure to do good things for Your children. Thank You, Lord. In Jesus' name, Amen.

# DAY 70
## Sunshine & Sunflowers

*Consider how the wild flowers grow. They do not labor or spin. Yet I tell you, not even Solomon in all his splendor was dressed like one of these. If that is how God clothes the grass of the field, which is here today, and tomorrow is thrown into the fire, how much more will he clothe you – you of little faith!*

**—LUKE 12:27-28 NIV**

I've always loved flowers. During the summer I am drawn to sunflowers. I love their big, bright petals but what really draws me to the flowers is their story. I learned as a child that sunflowers grow towards the sun. Even on cloudy days sunflowers will find the tiniest ray of sunlight peeking through the clouds and turn towards it. Instead of focusing on all the darkness, the sunflower seeks out that little light and faces it. It may not surprise you that sunflowers have somewhat of a thing for the sun. Even at night they're hankering for the light, turning their faces back east in the dark so they'll be ready to catch the first rays the moment dawn breaks. Sunflowers flourish when they are facing the sun. Isn't that just like us? When we are facing Jesus' light we are able to prosper and grow. Jesus said in John 8:12 "I am the light of the world. Whoever follows Me will not walk in darkness, but will have the light of life." Just like sunflowers, when we pray we are opening up from darkness into the light. Light reveals us to ourselves, which is not always so great if you find yourself in a big mess, possibly your own creation. But like sunflowers we turn toward light. Light warms and in most cases it draws us to itself. And in this light, we can see beyond shadow and illusion to something beyond our modest receptors, do what is truly deep down inside of us. Today, let's turn our backs on the darkness and face the brightness of Jesus' light. If you're going through a dark period in your life, know that God will be your ray of sunshine shining through the clouds that you need to turn your face towards healing, hope and grace. I hope the next time you see a sunflower you're reminded that when you turn your face toward the SON, you will receive the light you need to brighten your day and circumstances.

. . . . . . . . . . . . . . . . . . . . . . . . . . . . . . . . . . . . . . . . . . . . . . . . . . . . . . . . . . . . .

. . . . . . . . . . . . . . . . . . . . . . . . . . . . . . . . . . . . . . . . . . . . . . . . . . . . . . . . . . . . .

. . . . . . . . . . . . . . . . . . . . . . . . . . . . . . . . . . . . . . . . . . . . . . . . . . . . . . . . . . . . .

. . . . . . . . . . . . . . . . . . . . . . . . . . . . . . . . . . . . . . . . . . . . . . . . . . . . . . . . . . . . .

. . . . . . . . . . . . . . . . . . . . . . . . . . . . . . . . . . . . . . . . . . . . . . . . . . . . . . . . . . . . .

. . . . . . . . . . . . . . . . . . . . . . . . . . . . . . . . . . . . . . . . . . . . . . . . . . . . . . . . . . . . .

. . . . . . . . . . . . . . . . . . . . . . . . . . . . . . . . . . . . . . . . . . . . . . . . . . . . . . . . . . . . .

## Prayer for Today

O Lord, You are my hope when times are rough. When I encounter heavy burdens, You lift me up and give me a reason to hope for the future. Through You, my heart becomes filled with joy. I have faith that everything that happens is a part of Your plan. While I struggle under my burden, I know that you are there to support me and guide me through everything that happens. No matter what happens during this day, I know that Your everlasting joy will await me. Even when I struggle and face obstacles, I will feel happy knowing that I am doing Your bidding. Please bless me and help me to grow in my knowledge of You. In Jesus' name, I pray. Amen.

# DAY 71
# *Girl, Give It Up*

Better it is to be of a lowly in spirit with the oppressed than to share plunder with the proud.
**—PROVERBS 16:19 NIV**

The idea of control is such a funny thing. I admit, I am a recovering control freak. I never knew I was a control freak until talking with my sister one day. She was telling me how she was one also. Everything she described about herself was aligning with me as well. Me, a control freak? It couldn't be. I started to watch how I went about things and how I treated my husband and kids. I started to hear myself saying things like, "No, son you can't wear that tacky shirt, it clashes with your pants!" "Son, you can't go to that college, that campus experience is going to be awful." "Don't squeeze the ketchup bottle like that, do it this way!" "Honey, you need to give me more hugs and cuddle more, like this." "You can't eat tater tots for breakfast." Yep, the list goes on and on. It finally hit me. I am a bonafide control freak and didn't know it. Once I came to terms and admitted it, I did feel better. Sadly, everyone else around me said they already knew.

The bible says in Proverbs 19:21, "Many are the plans in the mind of a man, but it is the purpose of the Lord that will stand." And in Proverbs 16:9, "The heart of man plans his way, but the Lord establishes his steps." Straight from the book of wisdom. We plan, we prepare, we direct, and we strategize. We think we have everything organized and under "control". And then God smiles and shakes His head. He knows our future because He authored it. He knows our next move because He ordained it. Our sense of control over things in this life and on this earth is simple vanity. We want to be little gods over our little domain. In James 4:16 it's called "boasting in your arrogance." That's why I say I'm a recovering control freak. Once I realized how bad I wanted to be in charge of everything, I recognized it as sin. I don't need to control things, God has everything already under control. I shouldn't get in His way by thinking it's me getting things done right. I need to surrender the reins to Him. And honestly, what a relief that is. I don't have to direct my life, that's God's job. I just have to trust in Him and listen for His direction as I go. I also have to stay out of his way and allow Him to work in my husband's and my children's hearts as well. That's good, because as hard as I tried I couldn't fix them (yes, that's a joke). I just need to love them and encourage them to seek God's will too. Are you trying to control too much in your life? Give it up, girl! That's no way to live. Let your kids make life choices as long as it's not detrimental to their well-being. Their college experience is "their" experience, you've already experienced yours. Let your husband wear the stinky gym shorts. No one cares at 4:30 a.m in the gym anyways. Thank God for a husband who values physical and spiritual health and prays consistently. Ease up a little sis, it's not that serious.

. . . . . . . . . . . . . . . . . . . . . . . . . . . . . . . . . . . . . . . . . . . . . . . . . .

. . . . . . . . . . . . . . . . . . . . . . . . . . . . . . . . . . . . . . . . . . . . . . . . . .

. . . . . . . . . . . . . . . . . . . . . . . . . . . . . . . . . . . . . . . . . . . . . . . . . .

. . . . . . . . . . . . . . . . . . . . . . . . . . . . . . . . . . . . . . . . . . . . . . . . . .

. . . . . . . . . . . . . . . . . . . . . . . . . . . . . . . . . . . . . . . . . . . . . . . . . .

. . . . . . . . . . . . . . . . . . . . . . . . . . . . . . . . . . . . . . . . . . . . . . . . . .

. . . . . . . . . . . . . . . . . . . . . . . . . . . . . . . . . . . . . . . . . . . . . . . . . .

## Prayer for Today

God grant me the serenity to accept the things I cannot change; courage to change the things I can; and wisdom to know the difference. In Jesus' name, Amen.

# Just Be You

For You created my inmost being; You knit me together in my mother's womb. I praise You because I am fearfully and wonderfully made; your works are wonderful,

I know that full well.

**– PSALMS 139:13-14 NIV**

When God made you, He made you uniquely different from any other person on the planet. He had a specific purpose for your life even before you came here. God made you so special and uniquely different that your very fingerprint is unlike anyone else's in the world. Think about that. God took the time to create you in a way that when you call on Him in prayer, out of the multiple billions of people in the world He can distinguish the sound of your voice from all His other children. Isn't that a powerful thought? But the sad reality is that there are way too many of us trying to be imitators of others instead of embracing our own uniqueness. What a slap to the face of God for us to disregard our gift of authenticity and uniqueness out of a desire to mimic other people who seem to be more successful, more attractive, more wealthy or even more influential. You have gifts and talents that separate you from others. Yes there may be other people who do what you do but they are not you. You are fearfully and wonderfully made in the image and likeness of God the Father and Creator of the universe. If you have to constantly play up to people to convince them you're important then you are wasting valuable time. Great people usually recognize greatness in other people. You need to tell yourself, "I have something great to offer. I am one of a kind and I am not going to live my life trying to make people recognize my potential." Just be yourself. Everyone else is taken.

. . . . . . . . . . . . . . . . . . . . . . . . . . . . . . . . . . . . . . . . . . . . . . . . . .

. . . . . . . . . . . . . . . . . . . . . . . . . . . . . . . . . . . . . . . . . . . . . . . . . .

. . . . . . . . . . . . . . . . . . . . . . . . . . . . . . . . . . . . . . . . . . . . . . . . . .

. . . . . . . . . . . . . . . . . . . . . . . . . . . . . . . . . . . . . . . . . . . . . . . . . .

. . . . . . . . . . . . . . . . . . . . . . . . . . . . . . . . . . . . . . . . . . . . . . . . . .

. . . . . . . . . . . . . . . . . . . . . . . . . . . . . . . . . . . . . . . . . . . . . . . . . .

. . . . . . . . . . . . . . . . . . . . . . . . . . . . . . . . . . . . . . . . . . . . . . . . . .

## Prayer for Today

God I thank You for creating me uniquely different from anyone else in this world. Teach me how to walk in my uniqueness and embrace my authenticity so that I may effectively live on purpose and be who You called me to be. In Jesus' name, Amen.

# Choose Without Certainty

But blessed is the one who trusts in the Lord,
whose confidence is in him.
**– JEREMIAH 17:7 NIV**

When we're trying to make major decisions about our lives, the fear of making the wrong choice creates anxiety. We want to know without a doubt what we're supposed to do next. We'd often rather continue plodding down a familiar path than risk making a decision that could send us in a new, uncertain direction. We believe it's better to make no choice than the wrong choice. As a result, we become paralyzed by indecision and keep living the same story, unable to discern our calling for fear of making a mistake. For a long time, I have been traveling this road without much opposition. During my trip to Kampala, Uganda in the Mubende District there is a vast difference of roads. Roads that lead up the hill to the affluent, more wealthy district and another road that leads to the slums. These roads have gaps, dips, stones, dead animal carcasses, etc. The interesting thing is the roads that are rocky and filthy go to different pathways but you still have to travel on them whether you are going to the rich district or slums. You have to choose with uncertainty. Friend, you can have confidence and rest in the knowledge that if you're seeking God's will, He will redirect your path to take you where He wants you to go. Much like a GPS map recalculating our route when we take a wrong turn. Besides, detours can be a valuable part of the plan, revealing new things to us about ourselves, our calling, our world, and our Creator.

Day

# 73

. . . . . . . . . . . . . . . . . . . . . . . . . . . . . . . . . . . . . . . . . . . . . . . . . . . . .

. . . . . . . . . . . . . . . . . . . . . . . . . . . . . . . . . . . . . . . . . . . . . . . . . . . . .

. . . . . . . . . . . . . . . . . . . . . . . . . . . . . . . . . . . . . . . . . . . . . . . . . . . . .

. . . . . . . . . . . . . . . . . . . . . . . . . . . . . . . . . . . . . . . . . . . . . . . . . . . . .

. . . . . . . . . . . . . . . . . . . . . . . . . . . . . . . . . . . . . . . . . . . . . . . . . . . . .

. . . . . . . . . . . . . . . . . . . . . . . . . . . . . . . . . . . . . . . . . . . . . . . . . . . . .

. . . . . . . . . . . . . . . . . . . . . . . . . . . . . . . . . . . . . . . . . . . . . . . . . . . . .

## Prayer for Today

Loving God, we are made to be whole. I ask that You help me to become whole. Help me find the courage to be myself. Help me to find confidence in all my undertakings. Above all, grant me a clean bill of health and good results from my ultrasound so that I may do your work in the world. In Jesus' name I pray, Amen.

# DAY 74
## Brave Yet Afraid

David asked the soldiers standing nearby, "What will a man get for killing this Philistine and ending his defiance of Israel? Who is this pagan Philistine anyway, that he is allowed to defy the armies of the living God?

**—1 SAMUEL 17:26 NLT**

Do you feel brave? I am guessing your answer is "No" or "Not really." Don't worry, spoiler alert: most of us don't. The good news is feeling brave is not a requirement to acting brave. In fact, most people who achieve feats of bravery do not feel a magical sense of courage or bravery before they accomplish something. Brave is defined by Webster's dictionary as: "having or showing mental or moral strength to face danger, fear, or difficulty: having or showing courage." As Christians I believe we have supernatural strength on our side, but I rarely wake up feeling like it. Change is my least favorite thing and I am facing so much of it in my life right now. This includes my son heading off to college, becoming empty-nesters, starting a new role at my job and expanding our marriage ministry. I confess, all of it has me a little overwhelmed and nervous on how to take the next step with confidence. So what is this secret to bravery? I discovered it locked within the familiar story of David and Goliath. You've heard the ending before so you think you know where this is going, but maybe not. As I was reading in 1 Samuel 17, one particular verse stood out to me that I didn't remember ever reading before. Goliath, the intimidating giant warrior, has been coming out day after day taunting Israel and mocking their God while asking for someone to come fight him. Of course, every soldier is shaking in their boots and doesn't want to be destroyed so day after day no one accepts the invitation. Young teenager David arrives at the camp to visit his soldier brothers and sees Goliath doing his daily taunting. His response is what struck me in verse 26, "Who is this uncircumcised Philistine that he should defy the armies of the living God?" What a bold thing for David to say. I LOVE it! I asked myself, how could he say that instead of responding in fear like I always tend to do? Clearly, David knows the power of his God. Instead of looking at Goliath and running scared, he compared the size of Goliath to the size of his God and he could not be intimidated! This is the key to responding in bravery that many of us always miss. I keep my eyes focused on the problem in front of me and it seems so large compared to me, but compared to God EVERYTHING is small. If we change our view and put our trust in the right place, our living God will fight our battles for us. Hope in our own strength won't lead us to bravery, but hope in the omnipotent God will. Now go out there and conquer your Goliath with God on your side!

. . . . . . . . . . . . . . . . . . . . . . . . . . . . . . . . . . . . . . . . . . . . . . . . . . . . . . . . . . . . . .

. . . . . . . . . . . . . . . . . . . . . . . . . . . . . . . . . . . . . . . . . . . . . . . . . . . . . . . . . . . . . .

. . . . . . . . . . . . . . . . . . . . . . . . . . . . . . . . . . . . . . . . . . . . . . . . . . . . . . . . . . . . . .

. . . . . . . . . . . . . . . . . . . . . . . . . . . . . . . . . . . . . . . . . . . . . . . . . . . . . . . . . . . . . .

. . . . . . . . . . . . . . . . . . . . . . . . . . . . . . . . . . . . . . . . . . . . . . . . . . . . . . . . . . . . . .

. . . . . . . . . . . . . . . . . . . . . . . . . . . . . . . . . . . . . . . . . . . . . . . . . . . . . . . . . . . . . .

. . . . . . . . . . . . . . . . . . . . . . . . . . . . . . . . . . . . . . . . . . . . . . . . . . . . . . . . . . . . . .

## Prayer for Today

Lord, hide me in Your shelter. Be my refuge. I seek Your strength as I take this step of faith. Lord, there are things about this situation that are uncertain, but although I cannot see what's before me, I know You are with me. I am trusting You and walking in obedience with Your strength as my guide. I will no longer seek to hold tightly to a false sense of worth found in my fragile righteousness, nor in the wavering opinions of others. I will find my strength and my worth solely in You. I will seek You daily to feel the power of Your great love for me! I thank You for this strength and peace that comes from knowing I am Yours. In Jesus' name, Amen.

# You're An Overcomer

Little children, you are from God and have overcome them, for he who is in you is greater than he who is in the world.

**– 1 JOHN 4:4 NIV**

Nothing becomes great until it overcomes something. Paul writes, "For a great door has opened to me, and there are many adversaries" (1Co 16:9). Great doors of opportunity come with great challenges and those challenges will often stretch your faith. If outstanding success came easy, everybody would have it. But if everybody had it, then it wouldn't be outstanding success. How does a caterpillar develop into a butterfly? By overcoming the cocoon. Would it be easier to stay in the comfort of the cocoon? Some days the struggle is so great that the caterpillar probably thinks so. But the price of freedom, flight and discovery, is struggle, development and breakthrough. Why did Jesus send His disciples into the storm on the Sea of Galilee? To teach them to trust Him in every situation of life. Soon He'd be leaving them, so He used different experiences to equip them for the future.

What are you trying to overcome today? Instead of complaining about it, or asking God to take it away, try to see it as preparation for the thing He has called you to do. Read these Scriptures. "Blessed is the man who endures temptation" (James 1:12). "To him who overcomes I will give to eat from the tree of life" (Revelation 2:7). "Blessed are those who are persecuted for righteousness' sake, for theirs is the kingdom of heaven" (Matthew 5:10). "Be not overcome of evil, but overcome evil with good" (Romans 12:21). "Put on the whole armor of God, that ye may be able to stand against the wiles of the devil" (Ephesians 6:11). You're called to be an overcomer. The depth of your past is an indication of the height of your future. In other words, if you've been through a lot of negative things in the past, it just means that your future is bigger, brighter and greater than you can even imagine. Every day that you choose to lead and inspire greatness, you're an overcomer. Every day that you choose to not live in fear, you're an overcomer. Every day that you choose to be obedient to God's voice, you're an overcomer. Don't underestimate the power of being on a mission for God. You just might inspire greatness in someone else to become an overcomer along with you.

. . . . . . . . . . . . . . . . . . . . . . . . . . . . . . . . . . . . . . . . . . .

. . . . . . . . . . . . . . . . . . . . . . . . . . . . . . . . . . . . . . . . . . .

. . . . . . . . . . . . . . . . . . . . . . . . . . . . . . . . . . . . . . . . . . .

. . . . . . . . . . . . . . . . . . . . . . . . . . . . . . . . . . . . . . . . . . .

. . . . . . . . . . . . . . . . . . . . . . . . . . . . . . . . . . . . . . . . . . .

. . . . . . . . . . . . . . . . . . . . . . . . . . . . . . . . . . . . . . . . . . .

. . . . . . . . . . . . . . . . . . . . . . . . . . . . . . . . . . . . . . . . . . .

## Prayer for Today

Heavenly Father, thank You that Your grace is beyond measure. Throughout eternity, You have been working for my good and the good of all Your people. May I know Your power and grace to overcome the obstacles in my life. May the things that stand in my way become examples of Your limitless power. Clothe me with power as I live my life in Your righteous name. May I prosper and bring You glory on the earth. May I be steadfast, immovable, always abounding in the work of the Lord. Through Jesus Christ, our Lord. Amen.

# By Still Waters

He leads me by still waters.

**– PSALMS 23:2 NIV**

It all starts out peaceful and serene. The sound of birds singing, the warm rays of the sun shining through the window pane. The scent of freshly baked biscuits while breakfast is being prepared in the kitchen. It feels good to get out of bed in the morning. All indicators that it's gonna be a good day. And then you receive a text message or phone call with devastating news. All of a sudden what started out being a great start to your day spirals into a whirlwind. As you prepare to leave the house, you can't find your wallet or purse, you finally make it to your car and realize you are almost out of gas and the check engine light comes on. And just when you thought your day couldn't get any worse, your vehicle stalls out in rush hour traffic and you're gonna be late for work. It is in that exact moment you sense you are about to lose it and explode but somehow, some way you are overcome with a sense of peace and serenity. You hear in your spirit that everything will be okay and that God is in control. I don't know about you but there have been times in my life when I've gone from zero to one hundred in a matter of seconds. Anxiety, stress and tension takes control of my mind and I can't seem to shake it. There have also been times when everything on the outside is falling apart but on the inside God is carrying me through and I feel no sense of worry because He is guiding me to calm waters where I can gain a better perspective of His will for my life and His peace and protection for myself and my family. God is the Good Shepherd and we have to learn to let go of our sense of control and give Him the right of way to lead us and guide us into our rightful place in Him. As children of God we must realize that everyday is not going to be filled with sunshine, rainbows and roses. Some days we're going to feel defeated, depressed and depleted but God will never leave us nor forsake us. He never promised us we would not have trouble in this world but He did promise to be with us in the midst of our trouble. This is what keeps me grounded and confident. Knowing that God is taking me to and through places that are meant to build my character and to mold me into being who God has called me to be.

. . . . . . . . . . . . . . . . . . . . . . . . . . . . . . . . . . . . . . . . . . . . . . . . . . . . .

. . . . . . . . . . . . . . . . . . . . . . . . . . . . . . . . . . . . . . . . . . . . . . . . . . . . .

. . . . . . . . . . . . . . . . . . . . . . . . . . . . . . . . . . . . . . . . . . . . . . . . . . . . .

. . . . . . . . . . . . . . . . . . . . . . . . . . . . . . . . . . . . . . . . . . . . . . . . . . . . .

. . . . . . . . . . . . . . . . . . . . . . . . . . . . . . . . . . . . . . . . . . . . . . . . . . . . .

. . . . . . . . . . . . . . . . . . . . . . . . . . . . . . . . . . . . . . . . . . . . . . . . . . . . .

. . . . . . . . . . . . . . . . . . . . . . . . . . . . . . . . . . . . . . . . . . . . . . . . . . . . .

## *Prayer for Today*

God, I don't know what today holds but I know you hold my days in your hands. Give me the courage and confidence to be still, knowing You are leading me and guiding me by still waters and to a place of rest and reassurance in You. I am thankful for every setback, every season of frustration and turmoil because I know You can make it all work for my good. In Jesus' name, Amen

# DAY 77
## That Ain't Your Lane

To every thing there is a season and a time to every purpose under the heavens.
**—ECCLESIASTES 3:1 KJV**

If there's one thing I'm exceptionally good at doing, it's making excuses. Especially when it's something that I want to do even though God did not tell me to do it. Almost every man or woman in the Bible who was used by God to do incredible things started off with doubt, fear, impatience, stubbornness and even some control issues. There are plenty of instances of people's hearts being changed as they give God's plan a chance but it wasn't very easy in the beginning. Like Jonah, he thought he had a better way and went in the opposite direction of his purpose and ended up in the belly of a fish. One of the most reluctant in my opinion was Moses. Fearing for his life after a misguided attempt at being a freedom fighter, Moses retreated to Midian in his forties for some easy living in a remote country. Moses was hanging out in the countryside living his best life but not God's best. It wasn't long before God disrupted his life by calling him to leave his life of comfort to save his people from the hands of Pharaoh. It's here, in his first conversation with God, that we see Moses give excuse after excuse for why he could not do what God wanted him to do. While you may tell yourself that you would never have the audacity to reject God to His face, the truth is that you probably do this more often than you think. God is constantly pushing us through the scriptures to live lives filled with love and impact, and this can seem impossible, depending on your level of faith. However, there may be a reason why God is asking you to change lanes or even pull over. Could it be that God wants you to be obedient and He's showing you signs that He wants you to step out in faith? Remember, God knows the future and sometimes what He's asking you to do may seem impossible and outside of the norm. But in order for us to grow sometimes, He has to remove us from our comfort zone and recalculate your route.

## Day

# 77

. . . . . . . . . . . . . . . . . . . . . . . . . . . . . . . . . . . . . . . . . . . . . . . . . . . . . . . .

. . . . . . . . . . . . . . . . . . . . . . . . . . . . . . . . . . . . . . . . . . . . . . . . . . . . . . . .

. . . . . . . . . . . . . . . . . . . . . . . . . . . . . . . . . . . . . . . . . . . . . . . . . . . . . . . .

. . . . . . . . . . . . . . . . . . . . . . . . . . . . . . . . . . . . . . . . . . . . . . . . . . . . . . . .

. . . . . . . . . . . . . . . . . . . . . . . . . . . . . . . . . . . . . . . . . . . . . . . . . . . . . . . .

. . . . . . . . . . . . . . . . . . . . . . . . . . . . . . . . . . . . . . . . . . . . . . . . . . . . . . . .

. . . . . . . . . . . . . . . . . . . . . . . . . . . . . . . . . . . . . . . . . . . . . . . . . . . . . . . .

## Prayer for Today

Dear Heavenly Father, thank You for Your promise of provision. I know that You wouldn't lead me to a place where You won't provide for me. Help me to trust You even when things don't seem to be going right. Let me know when it's time to move and give me the faith to do Your will. Amen.

# Authentically YOU!

*When the Spirit of truth comes, he will guide you into all the truth, for he will not speak on his own authority, but whatever he hears he will speak, and he will declare to you the things that are to come.*

**– JOHN 16:13 ESV**

"The privilege of a lifetime is to become who you truly are" – Carl Jung. This quote sums up the importance of growing into your authentic self. Your authentic self is who you truly are as a person, regardless of your occupation, regardless of the influence of others, it is an unfiltered representation of you. To be authentic means not caring what others think about you. This may sometimes lead to standing out from the crowd. To be authentic is to be true to yourself, your thoughts, words and actions. It means being able to sacrifice any relationship, situation or circumstance that diverges from your truth. For example, if you're in a relationship or friendship that does not make you happy or makes you act differently from who you truly are, you might need to reevaluate your status. For some, it is a difficult task to define your authentic self because you don't just have one self; there are multiple versions of who you are. There is the self you are at work, the self you are with your best friends, the self you are with your family and the self you are among strangers. These "invented selves" are normal, and it's something we all have to do to some degree. Authenticity is not about expressing your opinions all the time without filters. It's about confidently knowing what those opinions are. Being authentic isn't just about being honest either. It's also about being self-aware, being humble and being open to receiving feedback from others. It is about answering introspective questions like "Who am I when no one is looking?" And "what would happen if I were to show up as that person?"

I have failed at times as a wife, daughter, mother, sister and friend. I don't always say the right things. I may not be the most beautiful woman in the world, but I am me. I have flaws. I have cellulite. I have scars because I have a history. Some people love me, some like me and some don't. I have done good. I have done bad. I go without makeup. Sometimes I don't do my hair. I'm random at times and silly but loving. I love people. I don't pretend to be someone I'm not. I am who I am. You can love me or not. And if I love you, I do with all my heart. I make no apologies for being me. Us becoming who we're meant to be isn't about being more of anything but ourselves. This awakening isn't something we can compare with another, as our journey differs from everyone else's. No one else can be a more authentic version of you than you. Your authentic self is already within you. Spiritual growth is about uncovering who we authentically are. Hear me when I say this, do not apologize for being YOU. Because you are amazing. You are fearfully and wonderfully made!

. . . . . . . . . . . . . . . . . . . . . . . . . . . . . . . . . . . . . . . . . . . . . .

. . . . . . . . . . . . . . . . . . . . . . . . . . . . . . . . . . . . . . . . . . . . . .

. . . . . . . . . . . . . . . . . . . . . . . . . . . . . . . . . . . . . . . . . . . . . .

. . . . . . . . . . . . . . . . . . . . . . . . . . . . . . . . . . . . . . . . . . . . . .

. . . . . . . . . . . . . . . . . . . . . . . . . . . . . . . . . . . . . . . . . . . . . .

. . . . . . . . . . . . . . . . . . . . . . . . . . . . . . . . . . . . . . . . . . . . . .

. . . . . . . . . . . . . . . . . . . . . . . . . . . . . . . . . . . . . . . . . . . . . .

## *Prayer for Today*

Lord, it can be so easy to keep our relationships with others at surface level. Our fears and insecurities prevent us from entering into those hard conversations and we go around masquerading fake smiles and endless pretenses but God, You know our thoughts before we even think them. You know all the hurt, the aches we can't identify and the longings for what's real. You go there, Lord, and You beckon us to come with You into the beautiful deep. God, help us to go there with You. Because when all the pretense melts away and we enter into that safe place, what we find is everything true, lovely and worth pursuing. In Jesus' name, Amen.

# Thankful

Praise the Lord. Give thanks to the Lord, for he is good; his love endures forever.

**– PSALM 106:1 NIV**

I have found that giving thanks for those things that are right in my life has given me the strength to deal with the adversities and setbacks that have popped up along the way. But there is another little secret that I have come to realize as I have gotten older, and that is that the greatest gifts I have received were the gifts of development, growth and resiliency. What is clear to me is that these gifts have made it possible to overcome the challenges and setbacks that I have faced along the way. The doors to the greatest opportunities were made available to me when the doors of rejection closed abruptly leaving me standing in the hallway waiting patiently for another door to open. To paraphrase the Dalai Lama, "Not getting what you want is sometimes a wonderful stroke of luck." Whether we ever understand why or why not, the only way through any unexpected shock is through. No matter how much we wish we could go around a situation, under it, over it or be delivered from it, there are times God wants to walk us through a process, because that is what's best for us. I've learned over time to celebrate and cherish it all. The highs, the lows, the blessings, the lessons, the setbacks, the comebacks and even the clap backs because they all challenged me to adapt, grow, learn and become stronger.

So take this quick moment before you move to Day 80 and pause and reflect on how your setbacks have served you well. Take an alternate approach to express your gratitude for all the good and bad things that have occurred in your life. There's always a hidden lesson within them. As you continue to pause and reflect, I'd like to challenge you to set your intentions on turning every test into a testimony and every mess into a message and remain grateful that your challenges are opportunities for growth.

. . . . . . . . . . . . . . . . . . . . . . . . . . . . . . . . . . . . . . . . . . . . . . . . . . . . . . . . . . . .

. . . . . . . . . . . . . . . . . . . . . . . . . . . . . . . . . . . . . . . . . . . . . . . . . . . . . . . . . . . .

. . . . . . . . . . . . . . . . . . . . . . . . . . . . . . . . . . . . . . . . . . . . . . . . . . . . . . . . . . . .

. . . . . . . . . . . . . . . . . . . . . . . . . . . . . . . . . . . . . . . . . . . . . . . . . . . . . . . . . . . .

. . . . . . . . . . . . . . . . . . . . . . . . . . . . . . . . . . . . . . . . . . . . . . . . . . . . . . . . . . . .

. . . . . . . . . . . . . . . . . . . . . . . . . . . . . . . . . . . . . . . . . . . . . . . . . . . . . . . . . . . .

. . . . . . . . . . . . . . . . . . . . . . . . . . . . . . . . . . . . . . . . . . . . . . . . . . . . . . . . . . . .

## Prayer for Today

Lord Jesus, forgive me for not saying "Thank You." I repent of focusing on the things I don't have, instead of the blessings You have given me. I want to be like the one who returned to express gratitude. Thank You for saving me, forgiving me and providing for my needs each day. In Jesus' name, Amen.

# Hello Little Girl

For we are his workmanship, created in Christ Jesus for good works, which God prepared before-hand, that we should walk in them.

**– EPHESIANS 2:10 ESV**

In 2021 I was selected to join this prestigious leadership fellows program for women and we were asked to do an exploratory assignment of sending a letter to our younger self. This was such an impactful experience that I wanted to incorporate this into my journal to hopefully inspire you to do the same. This is my letter I wrote to my younger self:

*Hello Kara Nicole,*

*This is a pivotal year for you because you are turning 13 and you're moving from your small rural town in Indiana, a place you lived for the first 12 years of your life to another unknown state, Oklahoma. Everything happens for a reason – – understand this move was purposeful. Without hurdles and obstacles, you would stay complacent and never learn or even grow. So, don't let fear dictate your pivots and try to push yourself outside of your comfort zone. The easy route is not always the best direction to go. Through every chapter, you will experience a new beginning so keep that half glass full mantra. Don't be so afraid of failure and don't worry about fitting in. So what if you're the only black girl and they make fun of you for "sounding white." Your diverse friendships and relationships will benefit you in the long run. Trust me on this. Kara, you're amazing, you were made for more, you're beautiful, confident and one of a kind. You have greatness within you and have tremendous value. Remember to know who you are but most importantly whose you are, which is a child of God. So, as you navigate through life, don't worry too much about the decisions you have to make. You will see those gut decisions do pay off in the long run, but don't rush your journey. Remember to listen to that inner voice and your parents, yes Carl and Katherine, and continue to stand up for what is right, ethical and important. Every step, every life turn and some U-turns were there for a reason. For you to either learn something new, try something new or stop and recalculate. When you look back over your journey, you will connect the mile markers and will hopefully smile. So remember, whatever you do, believe in yourself. You have untapped potential and you will accomplish everything you have dreamed about if you just try and jump in the deep.*

Now, the next challenge is to find an opportunity to plant a seed of encouragement with another young adult or teen. You may be the only Bible some people ever read.

. . . . . . . . . . . . . . . . . . . . . . . . . . . . . . . . . . . . . . . . . . . . . .

. . . . . . . . . . . . . . . . . . . . . . . . . . . . . . . . . . . . . . . . . . . . . .

. . . . . . . . . . . . . . . . . . . . . . . . . . . . . . . . . . . . . . . . . . . . . .

. . . . . . . . . . . . . . . . . . . . . . . . . . . . . . . . . . . . . . . . . . . . . .

. . . . . . . . . . . . . . . . . . . . . . . . . . . . . . . . . . . . . . . . . . . . . .

. . . . . . . . . . . . . . . . . . . . . . . . . . . . . . . . . . . . . . . . . . . . . .

## *Prayer for Today*

Dear Heavenly Father, Your word says that I am fearfully and wonderfully made. Your word also says that everything created by You is good and that nothing is to be rejected. Help me to be 100% of who You made me to be. I am made in Your image. Help my eyes to see, Lord. Give me the courage to walk in the world as my true self. Help me to be honest, truthful, real, and authentic. Kill the spirit of comparison in me. Direct me away from trying to be like anyone else. Forgive me, God for comparing myself and mimicking after anyone else. I know You have specific gifts and a specific purpose just for me. Lord, show me my gifts. Reveal to me my purpose. Make it plain, God, so I can write it on the tablets and run with it. Let me be Your vessel to lead Your people to living more fulfilling and purposeful lives. Help others heal where they need to heal and to grow where they need to grow. As they discover who they are, I pray that it leads them to you. I pray that they will be transformed by the renewing of their minds. In Jesus' name, Amen.

# Girl, Speak Up!

Open your mouth for the mute, for the rights of all who are destitute. Open your mouth, judge righteously, defend the rights of the poor and needy.

**– PROVERBS 31:8-9 ESV**

God's blessings to us are not meant to end with us. His desire is that they flow to others. One of the reasons I became a life coach was to help women, especially women of color navigate spaces and ecosystems by providing guidance, support, sisterhood and covering. Whether you have the professional status or the influence to be a true sponsor of someone's work, you can always opt in to advocate for a peer or colleague by shouting out their good work when you see it. One of the biggest acknowledgments you can give is to endorse their contributions in meetings by giving credit where credit is due. Literally it costs you nothing to mention good work when you see it, because when you do that you can literally shift the environmental work culture towards acknowledgement, amplification and positive reinforcement for women and specifically women of color in your professional network. But why as women, can't we consistently celebrate each other authentically and unapologetically without having any underlying motive? I often tell my mentees that there are enough seats at the table for all of us to sit comfortably. And if not, build your own table. But if you're like me, someone who is tired of sitting at the kid's table each and every year hoping to graduate or better yet get elevated, then allow this day to be your confirmation and you just say "screw it," and go to your nearest lumber store and get some planks of wood, a box of nails and rent a few power tools and start constructing your own table.

When you speak up, doors can open for you and for others. When you speak up, names can be brought forward. When you speak up, opportunities become attainable. As former U.S. First Lady Michelle Obama once said, "So many of us have gotten ourselves at the table, but we're still too grateful to be at the table to really shake it up. It'd be nice to have a collective of black women who are opening up spaces for each other, or making strategic moves to raise the visibility of black women within the industry, and not just who's on the cover of the magazine but behind the scenes too." Supporting women means you're being intentional about how you show up in life and business. Showing up means you're mentally present while listening and speaking up for yourself as well as others. Be an Esther in someone's life today because maybe you're in the role that you're in or have the title in front of your name for such a time as this! Take opportunities and moments that have been provided to you and reach back and pull someone forward. It is a blessing to be a blessing to others. Speak up and show up, girl!

. . . . . . . . . . . . . . . . . . . . . . . . . . . . . . . . . . . . . . . . . . . . . . . . . . . . .

. . . . . . . . . . . . . . . . . . . . . . . . . . . . . . . . . . . . . . . . . . . . . . . . . . . . .

. . . . . . . . . . . . . . . . . . . . . . . . . . . . . . . . . . . . . . . . . . . . . . . . . . . . .

. . . . . . . . . . . . . . . . . . . . . . . . . . . . . . . . . . . . . . . . . . . . . . . . . . . . .

. . . . . . . . . . . . . . . . . . . . . . . . . . . . . . . . . . . . . . . . . . . . . . . . . . . . .

. . . . . . . . . . . . . . . . . . . . . . . . . . . . . . . . . . . . . . . . . . . . . . . . . . . . .

. . . . . . . . . . . . . . . . . . . . . . . . . . . . . . . . . . . . . . . . . . . . . . . . . . . . .

## Prayer for Today

Dear Lord, I pray that I would use the authority You have given me to become Your mouthpiece on earth. Help me to pray breakthrough prayers under the leading of Your Holy Spirit. I thank You that positive confession brings breakthroughs. Ground me in Your word so that Your power can flow freely through my life like rivers of living water. Empower me to be and declare Your will, in Jesus' name, Amen.

# Can I Get A Selah?

Just as we have heard, so have we seen
In the city of the Lord of armies, in the city of our God;
God will establish her forever. Selah

**— PSALM 48:8 NASB**

Seventy-four times in the book of Psalms we see the word "Selah" at the end of a scripture. But what does it mean? Selah means to pause and calmly think about something. To reflect and meditate in the moment. When we think about all of the short stories throughout the Bible, one thing I have realized is that you can't rush into Bible revelation. And you can't skim the surface and discover the treasure hidden within without pausing, reflecting and allowing the word of God to breathe into your spirit. That's why David wrote, "With my whole heart have I sought thee: O let me not wander from thy commandments. Thy word have I hid in mine heart, that I might not sin against thee" (Psalms 119:10-11). When you hide God's Word in your heart through meditation and memorization, you're able to stand on it when you have a particular need. Meditation involves taking time to reflect; to pause and calmly think about something. It's a time-tested method God put in place for you. He wants you to learn to pray the scriptures and meditate on them because these habits will help you to experience all He has for you. The most important thing you can ask yourself when you face life's challenges is, "What does God say about this in His Word and why should this matter to me as a Christ-follower? When thinking about writing this journal entry, I found two scriptures, to help you get to the why. "Your word is settled in heaven" (Psalms 119:89). "The word of our God stands forever" (Isaiah 40:8).

God's word is His will. When God called Jeremiah to leadership, Jeremiah had reservations about his ability. So God said, "I have put My words in your mouth" (Jeremiah 1:9). Then He told Jeremiah, "I am ready to perform My word" (v. 12). The only thing you can count on for sure is that God will keep His Word. God always keeps His Word! The Bible says that, "He is not a man that He should lie." When God gives His Word to you, it's as good as done! The Word of God is what He has given you and the Bible says that, "All of the promises of God are yes and amen!" When you know that God keeps His Word, there is a rest in your spirit that it's as good as done! Can I get a Selah, somebody?

. . . . . . . . . . . . . . . . . . . . . . . . . . . . . . . . . . . . . . . . . . . . . . . . .

. . . . . . . . . . . . . . . . . . . . . . . . . . . . . . . . . . . . . . . . . . . . . . . . .

. . . . . . . . . . . . . . . . . . . . . . . . . . . . . . . . . . . . . . . . . . . . . . . . .

. . . . . . . . . . . . . . . . . . . . . . . . . . . . . . . . . . . . . . . . . . . . . . . . .

. . . . . . . . . . . . . . . . . . . . . . . . . . . . . . . . . . . . . . . . . . . . . . . . .

. . . . . . . . . . . . . . . . . . . . . . . . . . . . . . . . . . . . . . . . . . . . . . . . .

. . . . . . . . . . . . . . . . . . . . . . . . . . . . . . . . . . . . . . . . . . . . . . . . .

## Prayer for Today

Heavenly Father, As we rest in You, we ask that You would fill us with Your joy, abundance and peace. We ask that Your perfect wisdom would guide us to the right decisions. We ask that You would help us to show others that we meet the way into Your presence. Thank You Lord for Your promises and Your strong hand to lead and guide us. Please teach us Your ways and lead us into rest. We love You God and the way You care for us. In Jesus' name, Amen.

# DAY 83
# I Smell V-I-C-T-O-R-Y

"No, despite all these things, overwhelming victory is ours through Christ, who loved us."
**— ROMANS 8:37 NLT**

Our sense of smell is a powerful thing. The amazing thing about the sense of smell is we are able to detect with our noses the source of aromas without seeing it with our natural eyes. Without being told, for example, we know immediately when someone is baking cookies or that burgers are grilling on the stovetop simply by what we smell. We can tell when someone has just gotten out of the shower or is cleaning the house, because of the identifiable fragrances of soap. However, have you ever considered that God uses us to spread the aroma of the knowledge of Christ wherever we go too? That means that while being around us, people can sense Jesus without seeing Him. They can tell that God is in their midst because we showed up reflecting the love of Jesus Christ. The presence of the spirit of Christ within us impacts people. I need a victory over the darkness I feel creeping in. Do you ever feel that way? In times like this we need to worship God because worship can change the fragrance of any atmosphere. There are many ways to worship God, but today I am referring to praise through singing. Now, this may bring about images of church services or jamming out in your car (I often wonder if my kids know what the radio sounds like without me singing along to it). These are good, but let's break this wide open to understand some of the true power that can be released when we sincerely worship God. Let me tell you a true story that happened long ago. This story is found in 2 Chronicles chapter 20. Jehoshaphat was king of Judah and was facing a huge problem; a HUGE army in fact. Jehoshaphat had gotten word that an army from multiple countries was coming his way to make war with him and the people of Judah. They were vastly outnumbered and things looked bleak. The king sought help from the Lord. He ordered a fast and gathered the people of the nation together at the temple courtyard in Jerusalem. Jehoshaphat prayed to God, (see verses 6 – 12). The final lines of the prayer: "For we are powerless against this great horde that is coming against us. We do not know what to do, but our eyes are on you." (That last line is epic.)

While families stood together before the Lord, God spoke through a man named Jahaziel. He told King Jehoshaphat and the people of Judah not to be afraid of this vast army, "Do not be afraid and do not be dismayed at this great horde, for the battle is not yours, but God's." (v. 15). After this the people praised and worshiped God.

The worshipers were placed at the head of the army to praise God! When they began to sing, God acted and caused their enemies to fight against each other. By the time the army of Judah arrived, all were dead; that massive army of multiple countries was destroyed. God had fought the battle for them just as He said he would. Worship from a surrendered heart is undeniably powerful as it heightens the senses and creates a sweet aroma for the Holy Spirit to flow freely. When you praise and sing to God in sincerity it causes your heart to move nearer to God's heart. Worship is how we show our adoration for our God. It is a time of expression of His worthiness and greatness. It reminds us of our desperate need for Him. Worship places God back in His proper place as Lord of our life.

Ladies, I want you to remember this power the next time you begin to choke on life. Begin worshiping God with a sincere heart knowing that your words are reaching His ears and that He is working in your life and in your heart as you praise Him. No matter the battles you are facing or the discouragement you may be feeling, if Jesus is your Savior and Lord, you are headed to a great celebration of victory. You may not see it with your eyes, but God is using you and He is pleased to do so. You bring the good news of that victory with you wherever you go. Christ in you, the hope of glory!

. . . . . . . . . . . . . . . . . . . . . . . . . . . . . . . . . . . . . . . . . . . . . . . . . . . . . . . .

. . . . . . . . . . . . . . . . . . . . . . . . . . . . . . . . . . . . . . . . . . . . . . . . . . . . . . . .

. . . . . . . . . . . . . . . . . . . . . . . . . . . . . . . . . . . . . . . . . . . . . . . . . . . . . . . .

. . . . . . . . . . . . . . . . . . . . . . . . . . . . . . . . . . . . . . . . . . . . . . . . . . . . . . . .

. . . . . . . . . . . . . . . . . . . . . . . . . . . . . . . . . . . . . . . . . . . . . . . . . . . . . . . .

. . . . . . . . . . . . . . . . . . . . . . . . . . . . . . . . . . . . . . . . . . . . . . . . . . . . . . . .

. . . . . . . . . . . . . . . . . . . . . . . . . . . . . . . . . . . . . . . . . . . . . . . . . . . . . . . .

## Prayer for Today

Lord Jesus, there are many times that I don't feel like I'm winning. Fear and insecurity continue to plague me. But your Word points me to You, the cross and the empty tomb. The victory is assured. Help me always have my focus not on myself, but like Paul, on You. What a joy that I can confess: "I can do all things through Christ, who strengthens me." Amen.

# DAY 84
## Self Care is Not Selfish

Now listen to me, and let me give you a word of advice, and may God be with you. You should continue to be the people's representative before God, bringing their disputes to him.
**– EXODUS 18:19 NIV**

Last year, I realized that I lived 45 years around the sun without truly prioritizing my full wellness. Out of self-preservation, I would commonly respond to the question, How are you doing? with, "I can't complain," "I'm good", or "I'm blessed and highly favored" but truly on the inside I was broken, sad, stressed and full of anxiety. I was like a luxury boutique on the outside but the inside was a thrift shop. No, negative vibes to thrift shopping because I occasionally shop at thrift stores, but hopefully you get my point. I was known to have a stack of resiliency cards in my hand and I would often play them to avoid looking like I didn't have it all together and quite honestly I began to believe the lie. This strategy worked for almost a year until I was diagnosed with stress-induced shingles. For my 45th birthday, I started a 31 day self-care journey while making the proclamation that I was going to prioritize my wellness going forward and finally slow down and put on my own oxygen mask first before helping anyone else.

Self-care is not selfish. It's about doing things you initially don't want to do and making the choice to do what's uncomfortable. Self-care, as the word itself suggests, is what we do to take care of ourselves. We often associate self-care with indulgences, like a pedicure or a glass of wine after a long day. But self-care is about more than treating yourself. Self-care is the set of deliberate, healthy steps you take to maintain your physical, emotional and mental well-being. It includes things like nutrition, personal hygiene, exercise, relationships, and how we spend our leisure time. It's intentional, and it's important. It does not require an elaborate plan. It can be as simple as taking a deep breath when you notice you are becoming stressed. By maintaining your physical and mental health, you will likely be better equipped to handle the stressors that come along with supporting someone you care about. Developing a self-care routine is a simple but powerful way to invest in your mental and emotional health so you can continue to do the things that matter most. When we get stressed out, we tend to ignore the very things that might make us feel better, so it is important to find time to take care of yourself. It begins with accepting your personal failures then deciding to re-strategize them. It's not about giving in to your immediate urges when that means giving up on a long-term goal. It's about forgiving, letting go and accepting what you can't change. It's also about being willing to let people down and even saying goodbye to some of them. So what's the bottom line? What's the takeaway here? Genuine self-care involves recognizing and accepting your imperfections while also finding ways to improve yourself compassionately. It also often means making compromises and recognizing that no compromise is perfect.

For me, my self-care journey started with prayer then moved into taking some intentional steps. Like any other skill, self-care requires finding a routine that works best for you.

Here are a few kick-starters to start your own personal self-care journey, today.

1. Acknowledge things are hard but you don't have to master them all in one day.
2. Scale back. It is ok to say NO to some things and people.
3. Make time for the things you love that make you smile.
4. Control the controllables.
5. Daily prioritize your mind, body and soul.

. . . . . . . . . . . . . . . . . . . . . . . . . . . . . . . . . . . . . . . . . . . . . . . . . . . . . . . . . . . . . . .

. . . . . . . . . . . . . . . . . . . . . . . . . . . . . . . . . . . . . . . . . . . . . . . . . . . . . . . . . . . . . . .

. . . . . . . . . . . . . . . . . . . . . . . . . . . . . . . . . . . . . . . . . . . . . . . . . . . . . . . . . . . . . . .

. . . . . . . . . . . . . . . . . . . . . . . . . . . . . . . . . . . . . . . . . . . . . . . . . . . . . . . . . . . . . . .

. . . . . . . . . . . . . . . . . . . . . . . . . . . . . . . . . . . . . . . . . . . . . . . . . . . . . . . . . . . . . . .

. . . . . . . . . . . . . . . . . . . . . . . . . . . . . . . . . . . . . . . . . . . . . . . . . . . . . . . . . . . . . . .

. . . . . . . . . . . . . . . . . . . . . . . . . . . . . . . . . . . . . . . . . . . . . . . . . . . . . . . . . . . . . . .

## Prayer for Today

Lord, lift me up for Your blessings today. I pray that You will anoint me with strength and self care today, tomorrow and always. I pray that You will grace me with patience and wisdom. I pray that You will encourage me throughout the day to take the correct steps to walk proudly and behave well. I pray for all of these things in Jesus' name, Amen.

# *Get On Up!*

Even if good people fall seven times, they will get back up. But when trouble strikes the wicked, that's the end of them.

**– PROVERBS 24:16 CEV**

In the famous lyrics of one of my favorite 90's R&B boy bands, Jodeci "You gotta get on up, girl, now you can't sit down!" If you have ever seen a child learning to walk, you know that falling down is an inevitable part of the process. Falling down and getting back up is crucial to establishing the child's balance and muscle development. Likewise, in a boxing match, a fighter isn't disqualified because he gets knocked down; he's disqualified because he doesn't get back up. It's all about getting up over and over again. The Bible tells us that falling is common to both the righteous and unrighteous. It's getting up again that sets them apart: If good people fall, they will get back up. But when trouble strikes the wicked, that's the end of them. The unrighteous stay down, the righteous get up again! In scripture, some of God's greatest servants fell into personal failure. Jacob deceived his father and stole his brother's birthright (Genesis 27:17-29). Yet instead of being disqualified, they "were all commended for their faith" (Hebrews 11:39 NIV). Why? Because they acknowledged their sin and received God's forgiveness. In other words, they fell, but they got up again. And when you fall, you can get up again too. If you find yourself at the point of giving up today, encourage yourself to get back up again. You are worth the effort it takes to get to your expected end. You are worth the fight that it takes to move from a place of mediocrity and begin living the life you were destined to live. There is hope for you. That's the "faith" part of your journey. Staying down is failure accepted but getting back up is activating your faith!

· · · · · · · · · · · · · · · · · · · · · · · · · · · · · · · · · · · · · · · · · · · · · · · · · · · · · ·

· · · · · · · · · · · · · · · · · · · · · · · · · · · · · · · · · · · · · · · · · · · · · · · · · · · · · ·

· · · · · · · · · · · · · · · · · · · · · · · · · · · · · · · · · · · · · · · · · · · · · · · · · · · · · ·

· · · · · · · · · · · · · · · · · · · · · · · · · · · · · · · · · · · · · · · · · · · · · · · · · · · · · ·

· · · · · · · · · · · · · · · · · · · · · · · · · · · · · · · · · · · · · · · · · · · · · · · · · · · · · ·

· · · · · · · · · · · · · · · · · · · · · · · · · · · · · · · · · · · · · · · · · · · · · · · · · · · · · ·

· · · · · · · · · · · · · · · · · · · · · · · · · · · · · · · · · · · · · · · · · · · · · · · · · · · · · ·

## *Prayer for Today*

Father, even the disciples that walked with Jesus needed to strengthen their faith. Jesus told them if their faith was only the size of a mustard seed, they could uproot trees and crumble mountains. Lord, I need more faith like the disciples. Increase my faith and make me a mover of mountains. Grow my belief in You alone so that I would be strong in You and ready to battle against the doubts planted by the enemy. Lord, increase my faith! Help me get back up again, in Jesus' name, Amen.

# You're a WHOLE V.I.B.E.

Her children arise and call her blessed; her husband also, and he praises her:
"Many women do noble things, but you surpass them all."
**– PROVERBS 31: 28-29 NIV**

I assume when you were growing up your parents like mine would always remind you to be a leader, not a follower. We were always taught to be leaders but we live in a world today where being a leader is somewhat frowned upon in many settings. The world is constantly telling us that we must follow the new trends, new norms and that we must adjust who we are so we can be a part of the popular culture. Everyone of us wants to feel accepted. Everybody wants to be loved and acknowledged. None of us like to be rejected. Rejection is like the death of the soul.

The first rule in leadership is understanding that you are a misfit. You don't fit in with the crowd but you fit uniquely into God's plan. You're a masterpiece in the making! Culture might try to dictate your value and purpose, but God says you are a whole V.I.B.E.– **VICTORIOUS. INCREDIBLE. BLESSED. EXCEPTIONAL**.

We were never meant to find our own purpose on this earth. Rather, our purpose is to recognize we are made in the image of God to reflect His love and work toward His purpose. Why is it so crucial that we identify that we were made in God's image? Recognizing that we were created in God's image enables us to allow God to manifest Himself in and through us entirely. Seeking our purpose on our own is trying to discover what we were made for in and through us, which misses the fact that our purpose is in Christ. There are certainly two types of leaders: those that light up a room when they walk into it and those that make a room light up when they walk out of it. The former are radiators; the latter drainers.

Ultimately in the leadership stakes, the chief currency is energy; how you deploy it and how you distribute it. Don't compromise your convictions or character. If you don't stand for something, you'll fall for anything. Every great leader stands for something. Don't be afraid to say NO! Don't sell out on your morals and values. Be sold out to Christ! Keep standing for God. Continue to be an example for others even when it gets hard. You never know who is looking up to you and being inspired by you. Being a leader means being lonely at times. But stay on the right track and keep living a life that pleases, honors and glorifies God.

Today, I encourage you to own your differences, tune out the negative voices and don't sell out to the culture. Lead the crowd. Be yourself. Make the right decisions. Don't let anyone pressure you to do wrong. Seek God and strive to be a model for others to follow. The world is watching you. Your difference will put you on display. People know when you're not being yourself. You can't please everybody but you can please God and yourself. My friend, it's time to stand out because you're a whole vibe in Jesus Christ!

. . . . . . . . . . . . . . . . . . . . . . . . . . . . . . . . . . . . . . . . . . . . . . . . . . . . . .

. . . . . . . . . . . . . . . . . . . . . . . . . . . . . . . . . . . . . . . . . . . . . . . . . . . . . .

. . . . . . . . . . . . . . . . . . . . . . . . . . . . . . . . . . . . . . . . . . . . . . . . . . . . . .

. . . . . . . . . . . . . . . . . . . . . . . . . . . . . . . . . . . . . . . . . . . . . . . . . . . . . .

. . . . . . . . . . . . . . . . . . . . . . . . . . . . . . . . . . . . . . . . . . . . . . . . . . . . . .

. . . . . . . . . . . . . . . . . . . . . . . . . . . . . . . . . . . . . . . . . . . . . . . . . . . . . .

. . . . . . . . . . . . . . . . . . . . . . . . . . . . . . . . . . . . . . . . . . . . . . . . . . . . . .

## Prayer for Today

Dear Heavenly Father, I believe there is freedom through Your son Jesus Christ. He is my Savior, my Rock, and my Redeemer. I want to tell everyone I know about the renewed life found through a relationship with Him but I feel like I lack the boldness to do what You've called me to do. Help me have boldness through the power of Your Holy Spirit. Thank You for making this incredible power available to us. Thank You that with the Holy Spirit leading us, we can live with boldness for You. In Jesus' name we pray, Amen.

# The Genesis Prayer

In the beginning God created the heavens and the earth.
**– GENESIS 1:1 NIV**

It's not about you. The purpose of your life is far greater than your own personal fulfillment, your peace of mind or even your happiness. It's far greater than your family, your career or even your wildest dreams and ambitions. If you want to know why you were placed on this planet, you must begin with God. You were born by His purpose and for His purpose. The search for the purpose of life has puzzled people for generations. That's because we typically begin at the wrong starting point, ourselves. We ask self-centered questions like "What do I want to be? What should I do with my life? What are my goals, my ambitions, my dreams for my future?" But focusing on ourselves will never reveal our life's purpose. The Bible says, "It is God who directs the lives of his creatures; everyone's life is in his power" Job 12:10 GNT. Contrary to what many popular books, movies, and seminars tell you, you won't discover your life's purpose by looking within yourself. You've probably tried that already. You didn't create yourself, so there is no way you can tell yourself what you were created for. If I handed you an invention you had never seen before, you wouldn't know its purpose and the invention itself wouldn't be able to tell you either. Only the creator or the owner's manual could reveal its purpose.

I once got lost on my way to the office, yes it was my first week going to a new building. No judgment. When I stopped to ask for directions to the office, I was told, "You can't get there from here without waiting hours in traffic." In the same way, you cannot discover your life's purpose by starting with a focus on yourself. You must begin with God, your Creator. You exist only because God wills that you exist. You were made by God and for God and until you understand that, life will never make sense. It is only in God that we discover our origin, our identity, our meaning, our purpose, our significance and our destiny. Every other path leads to a dead end. Many people try to use God for their own self-actualization but that is a reversal of nature and is doomed to fail. You were made for God, not vice versa, and life is about letting God use you for His purposes, not your using Him for your own purpose. Once I realized that, it was life-changing and I truly began to live on purpose with intentionality. When did it all begin for you? When did you have your lightbulb moment? Retrace your steps and go back to the beginning; God. There are usually answers and clues waiting for you.

........................................................

........................................................

........................................................

........................................................

........................................................

........................................................

........................................................

## *Prayer for Today*

Holy Spirit, create in me a clean heart that seeks the best in others. Help me to show empathy and compassion to everyone, and to do so with gentleness and respect. When people or circumstances don't meet my expectations, empower me to show grace and understanding. Help me to see my situations from Your perspective so that I can rejoice at all times and show patience when needed. In Jesus' name, Amen.

# DAY 88
## Whoa — Man, Slow Down!

Martha, Martha," the Lord answered, "you are worried and upset about many things, but few things are needed—or indeed only one. Mary has chosen what is better, and it will not be taken away from her."

**– LUKE 10:41-42 NIV**

Hey, woman of God! It's time to take it down a notch and chill for a second. I get it. It's easy to get busy in life and if you're like me, you can listen and work at the same time. We call it "multi-tasking," but sometimes multitasking isn't the best use of our time. I know you're excited to fulfill your purpose, but God didn't call you to try to accomplish everything in a year. God wants to make you rich in experiences. He is showing you how to have a life that is abundant. In the world today, we are mostly in a hurry. We are busy people, constantly pursuing, attaining and launching something. We accomplish one feat and then we are on to the next one with no time set apart to process what God just did or to receive clear instructions from Him. We become like Joshua at the battle of Ai. After God delivered the city of Jericho into his hands in grand style, he assumed the city of Ai would be no different. He didn't seek God for His plan or His instructions and was chased down the mountain by the men he and his army went in to defeat; their hearts melting like water. After public humiliation, he cried out to God and He gave Him instructions and the victory.

The secret to success in God is in our constantly seeking Him. He tells us that when we diligently seek Him, we shall be rewarded. Our reward is victory. Our reward is Him being glorified in our lives. So let's slow down my sister. Do we want to be busy or do we want to be effective? Now that will preach! Do we want to constantly try our own methods or do we want a sweatless anointing that glorifies God? I believe, if you're like me, you want 100% or close to 100% effectiveness. You want God to be glorified in everything you set out to do by His grace. You want total victory. You want to please Him and the only thing that pleases Him is our faith, which comes by hearing what He wants you to do and doing it. Nothing more, nothing less.

*Day*

## 88

. . . . . . . . . . . . . . . . . . . . . . . . . . . . . . . . . . . . . . . . . . . . . . . . . . . . . .

. . . . . . . . . . . . . . . . . . . . . . . . . . . . . . . . . . . . . . . . . . . . . . . . . . . . . .

. . . . . . . . . . . . . . . . . . . . . . . . . . . . . . . . . . . . . . . . . . . . . . . . . . . . . .

. . . . . . . . . . . . . . . . . . . . . . . . . . . . . . . . . . . . . . . . . . . . . . . . . . . . . .

. . . . . . . . . . . . . . . . . . . . . . . . . . . . . . . . . . . . . . . . . . . . . . . . . . . . . .

. . . . . . . . . . . . . . . . . . . . . . . . . . . . . . . . . . . . . . . . . . . . . . . . . . . . . .

. . . . . . . . . . . . . . . . . . . . . . . . . . . . . . . . . . . . . . . . . . . . . . . . . . . . . .

### Prayer for Today

Yes, Father, I hear You loud and clear. I love doing what you've called me to do, but help me to slow down and receive instructions from You. I can do nothing in my own ability. I am desperately and hopelessly dependent on You. I want to be effective, not busy. I want victory and for You to be glorified. Help me to consistently seek You and not lean on my own understanding. Thank You for this precious blessing. In Jesus' name, Amen.

# It's Okay To Not Be Okay

Many are the afflictions of the righteous, but the Lord delivers him out of them all.
**– PSALM 34:19**

I have found during my seasoned years of life that most of us have mastered the art of pretending that we don't have any struggles or any junk or baggage in our lives. Oftentimes we want others to think we are on top of the mountain all of the time, but the truth of it all is, we're not. In fact, I get a lot of freedom from saying, "it's okay to not be okay."

I want to feel a different kind of peace. The peace that comes from our Creator. It's not my job to lie and create the perfect image of myself so others think nothing is wrong. It's okay if I am struggling. It's okay to ask for help from others. I need to be vulnerable and to accept the times in which I fail. It's okay to look bad and that's the most humbling thing I can tell myself. Christ forgives me and in my chaos the Sustainer brings peace.

It wasn't John the Baptist's appearance that brought the crowds of people. No, it was the need for people to find freedom. I can imagine what the people of Jerusalem could be feeling at that moment. The anticipation of wanting to be free of the junk. John's message was simple: that repentance is the way to the forgiveness of sins. John gives the people and us a very important message. Not only will they be baptized with water, but with the Holy Spirit. This message of empowerment is an important reminder that not only will we be forgiven if we ask, but that we are filled with the Holy Spirit allowing us to live devoted lives.

. . . . . . . . . . . . . . . . . . . . . . . . . . . . . . . . . . . . . . . . . . . . .

. . . . . . . . . . . . . . . . . . . . . . . . . . . . . . . . . . . . . . . . . . . . .

. . . . . . . . . . . . . . . . . . . . . . . . . . . . . . . . . . . . . . . . . . . . .

. . . . . . . . . . . . . . . . . . . . . . . . . . . . . . . . . . . . . . . . . . . . .

. . . . . . . . . . . . . . . . . . . . . . . . . . . . . . . . . . . . . . . . . . . . .

. . . . . . . . . . . . . . . . . . . . . . . . . . . . . . . . . . . . . . . . . . . . .

. . . . . . . . . . . . . . . . . . . . . . . . . . . . . . . . . . . . . . . . . . . . .

## Prayer for Today

Loving God, please grant me peace of mind and calm my troubled heart. I trust your love God, and I know that you will heal this stress. In Jesus' name, Amen.

# Dream Killers

Being confident of this, that he who began a good work in you will carry it on to completion until the day of Christ Jesus.

**– PHILLIPIANS 1:6 NIV**

Have you ever shared your dreams with someone and they crushed them? Getting closer to realizing your dreams is a challenging task on its own. However, take my word on this, be leary of those around you who are dream killers! They try to immobilize your life and put you in a place of bondage. But dream killers aren't only people. It can be less material factors such as fear, past failures or exhaustion. All of these take a great toll on your life and make it more difficult to reach your life goals. There are dreams within you. One of the greatest gifts you have in your life is the ability to see beyond your present state and dream. It is all about God's great purposes and plans He has designed for you. No one can define your dream but you. God gives your dream to you alone. So what will become of your dream? Will you decline it? Will you develop it? Will you give birth to it? Will you go through the process? Who do you share your dreams and goals with? It's time to take a closer look at your associates and friends or risk being heartbroken. Nelson Mandala once said "if you're playing small, you're playing selfish." The last thing the world needs is for someone to play small. Pursue the dream God has put in your life. There's no difference between your "true" self and God's plan for you. Your true self is made up of your deepest desires and gifts and abilities and dreams and passions. Your true self is what God created in you. It is who God made you to be. Instead of accepting the limits that have been placed on you, including the limits you have placed on yourself, pursue your passion!

Dreams come to pass when we step out and challenge life and take on the possibilities that lie before us. So keep on dreaming. You can do it. You can give birth to it. Whatever you do, don't stop! However, some of you can't keep things to ourselves. If you're one of these folks, my advice is always share your testimonies and not your plans because you never know the thoughts going on in the mind of that person you are discussing your future plans with. So always be as "gentle as a dove and as wise as a serpent" when it comes to divulging dreams and aspirations. Therefore be confident that God will complete what He has started in you (Philippians 1:6). You don't need to know everything. You may never know much of anything. But make sure you know that the same God who gave you your dream, who transformed you and made you a new creation, this same God will bring His work to completion. Now is the time to dream with no limitations and with no ceilings. Live your greatest life!

. . . . . . . . . . . . . . . . . . . . . . . . . . . . . . . . . . . . . . . . . . . . . . . . . . . .

. . . . . . . . . . . . . . . . . . . . . . . . . . . . . . . . . . . . . . . . . . . . . . . . . . . .

. . . . . . . . . . . . . . . . . . . . . . . . . . . . . . . . . . . . . . . . . . . . . . . . . . . .

. . . . . . . . . . . . . . . . . . . . . . . . . . . . . . . . . . . . . . . . . . . . . . . . . . . .

. . . . . . . . . . . . . . . . . . . . . . . . . . . . . . . . . . . . . . . . . . . . . . . . . . . .

. . . . . . . . . . . . . . . . . . . . . . . . . . . . . . . . . . . . . . . . . . . . . . . . . . . .

. . . . . . . . . . . . . . . . . . . . . . . . . . . . . . . . . . . . . . . . . . . . . . . . . . . .

## *Prayer for Today*

Lord God, You help me when I seek You. You are the ever-near friend in my time of trouble. I ask You to walk with me every step of my life. Though I will find many dark places and challenges that will make me feel like giving up, with You I will be confident and I will be strong. With You, I will not be afraid to move forward. You are my strength and my rock. Amen.

# DAY 91
## O.T.G.

Jesus Christ is the same yesterday, today, and forever.
**—HEBREWS 13:8 NLT**

The older I get, the more I appreciate timeliness. People who show up on time, whether it's for church, work or other events, give others the respect of their time and energy. Those who come consistently late seem to lack appreciation for what others have to do in their absence or tardiness. I have been on both sides. Being early and late. So I've learned to work on my time management. While we may be early or late, I am thankful to have an O.T.G. aka an "on time God". However, it took a long time to accept the fact that my timing is not always His timing and His schedule is not always in sync with my schedule. When we pray, we want God to move right away. Yet most of the time, it doesn't happen that way. In fact, sometimes it may seem to get worse before it gets better. Yet after a while, our faith gets stretched and weathered as we learn to trust in God's perfect timing. But why does He seem to wait until the eleventh hour? Well, here's a hard pill to swallow my friend. God's ways are not our ways. We can only see our side of things while God sees everyone and everything around our situation. Our God is sovereign and all-powerful. He can make pathways cross between people we could never imagine. We tend to think a lot about our situations and all the different options that could work out. Yet our God isn't limited by our possibilities. Rather, He has impossibilities that can come together right on time. Remember, God's timing isn't our timing. We get in a hurry for what we think should happen right away. God doesn't live in our finite human time. He is eternal. One day is like a thousand years, and a thousand years is like one day for God (2 Peter 3:8). Remember, God's plans aren't our plans. We can make our plans, but we don't have the control to make everything happen as we want. God has plans for us that are for our good, even when we don't understand how it's all going to work together.

. . . . . . . . . . . . . . . . . . . . . . . . . . . . . . . . . . . . . . . . . . . . . . . . . . . . . . .

. . . . . . . . . . . . . . . . . . . . . . . . . . . . . . . . . . . . . . . . . . . . . . . . . . . . . . .

. . . . . . . . . . . . . . . . . . . . . . . . . . . . . . . . . . . . . . . . . . . . . . . . . . . . . . .

. . . . . . . . . . . . . . . . . . . . . . . . . . . . . . . . . . . . . . . . . . . . . . . . . . . . . . .

. . . . . . . . . . . . . . . . . . . . . . . . . . . . . . . . . . . . . . . . . . . . . . . . . . . . . . .

. . . . . . . . . . . . . . . . . . . . . . . . . . . . . . . . . . . . . . . . . . . . . . . . . . . . . . .

. . . . . . . . . . . . . . . . . . . . . . . . . . . . . . . . . . . . . . . . . . . . . . . . . . . . . . .

## *Prayer for Today*

God of grace, I am thankful that I can count on Your unchanging ways. You are always loving, merciful and full of grace. Thank You for always being there for me. Thank You for consistently being in my midst when I struggle. In Jesus' name, Amen.

# Hidden Potential

For no word from God will ever fail.
**— LUKE 1:37 NIV**

Have you ever felt God calling you to something? How did you react? Did you cautiously tiptoe toward the calling or zealously run out in front of the calling?

Maybe you compared your qualifications and skill set with the job description, only to determine that you don't have what it takes on paper. Perhaps your heart leaped for joy at the prospect of being called to do something in ministry. The moment quickly turned from joy to sadness as your mind replayed the highlight reel of all the times you've failed and every fault that previously held you back from success. A sick feeling rushes from the bottom of your feet to the top of your head and fear overtakes your thoughts. If you survey the Who's Who of the Movers and Shakers of the Bible, you will discover they felt the same way as you and I. In fact, God has a history of selecting individuals who felt weak, underqualified, disqualified and unworthy. But God is a God who specializes in using the underdog—the least likely to succeed—to accomplish His purposes. So go ahead, let out a big sigh of relief. You and I get to rub elbows with the likes of some of the greats—people who shied away from the invitation to be part of God's incredible narrative. Here's the thing, we don't have to believe in our potential—we just have to believe in the God who sees our potential. God doesn't care that you failed a thousand times before. He's not concerned that you don't have a higher education. He's willing to help you overcome the faults that bring you down and the fear that keeps you up at night. He's the God who sees, El Roi. You are a worthwhile possibility and you are valuable. He sees you that way too. The word potential is defined as "present but not yet visible, apparent, or actualized, excellence or ability that may or may not be developed; possible, as opposed to actual." A person with potential is someone who is a worthwhile possibility. God may not call you to deliver a nation from bondage but I promise what He has in store for you is no less significant to the advancement of His kingdom. Therefore, never forget you are a worthwhile possibility. He hasn't forgotten you. You have something to offer that no one else has. God is the only one who knows how much we can achieve or who we can become.

. . . . . . . . . . . . . . . . . . . . . . . . . . . . . . . . . . . . . . . . . . . . . . .

. . . . . . . . . . . . . . . . . . . . . . . . . . . . . . . . . . . . . . . . . . . . . . .

. . . . . . . . . . . . . . . . . . . . . . . . . . . . . . . . . . . . . . . . . . . . . . .

. . . . . . . . . . . . . . . . . . . . . . . . . . . . . . . . . . . . . . . . . . . . . . .

. . . . . . . . . . . . . . . . . . . . . . . . . . . . . . . . . . . . . . . . . . . . . . .

. . . . . . . . . . . . . . . . . . . . . . . . . . . . . . . . . . . . . . . . . . . . . . .

## *Prayer for Today*

Father, I thank You that You created our potential. So for those who don't know You, God, I pray You would draw them near. Bring them in. Let them come to know You as all-in-all so they may find their all in You. And for those who do know You, God, I ask You to allow us to know You more. As we know You more, we learn more about Your ways and Your desires. As we learn more about You, we love You more. We love our neighbor more. And our lives will line up with Your deep desires for our lives. And Father, for those who don't see their potential, whose eyes the enemy has blinded, I ask You to grant wisdom and vision. Let them throw off the old and burst forth into the new. Let their lives push past the pain and take hold of the promise. We press toward our true potential, the mark of our high and holy calling in Christ Jesus, in whose glorious name I pray, Amen.

# Beloved, You're Forgiven

Under the old covenant, the priest stands and ministers before the altar day after day, offering the same sacrifices again and again, which can never take away sins. But our High Priest offered himself to God as a single sacrifice for sins, good for all time. Then he sat down in the place of honor at God's right hand. There he waits until his enemies are humbled and made a footstool under his feet. For by that one offering he forever made perfect those who are being made holy.

**– HEBREWS 10:11-14 NLT**

If you have accepted the gift of salvation from Jesus Christ, your sins have all been paid in full. You don't need a minister dressed in black with a white collar or a priestly robe to tell you this. The one and only man who walked this earth who could redeem you and pay the penalty for sin did so long ago. Job done. Period. The forgiveness of sin happened at only one point on our human timeline of history and that was on the cross of Calvary by Jesus Christ years ago. His blood poured out as He consumed the full wrath of his Father (the wrath we deserved). He gave up His spirit as He declared, "It is finished!" John 19:30. This is the moment when the sin of the world was forgiven. Mission accomplished. Jesus paid for your sins and mine at that exact moment. It is imperative that you understand this if you are a believer. Never minimize the sacrifice of our Jesus dying in our place. If you think you can say enough repetitive prayers or do enough good works to earn forgiveness, you are gravely mistaken and in attempting to do so, it's like spitting in the face of Jesus. If His act was lacking, then we would have to crucify the Son of God over and over again to accomplish forgiveness multiple times. What a worthless and insufficient god that would be.

Beloved, do not fall prey to that deceived way of thinking. If you have accepted Jesus, have turned from your life of sin, and now live for Him, you are forgiven. Your sins have been washed away by the all sufficient blood of Jesus Christ. This is what causes us Christians to love our Savior so much and provokes us to worship Him with unreserved gratitude. Is repentance still needed? Heck, yeah! When your eyes are opened to your sins and you see that they are what keep you from a loving God, you will fall on your knees with a contrite heart seeking mercy and forgiveness. "If we confess our sins, he is faithful and just to forgive us our sins and to cleanse us from all unrighteousness." 1 John 1:9. After salvation will we still sin? Heck, yeah! It is a daily battle, but the price Jesus paid is still good. Paid in full, no take backs.

Friends, when Jesus died, the veil in the temple that separated the Holy Place from the Most Holy Place (where only the high priest was allowed to go once per year to atone for the sins of the people) was torn in two from top to bottom (Matthew 27:51). No more earthly intercessors needed. We have full access granted to the mercy of God because of what Jesus did. Now, that is good news. If you have not yet done so, seek His mercy and turn to God today. If you have received this mercy, you are familiar with the awesomeness of this forgiveness that I speak of. Praise God for it! Your freedom has been granted. Walk in the victory that Christ has provided, knowing your debt has been paid in full! If you are still uncertain of your salvation, pray this prayer with me:

Dear God, I know I'm a sinner and I ask for Your forgiveness. I believe Jesus Christ is Your Son. I believe that He died for my sin and that you raised Him to life. I want to trust Him as my Savior and follow Him as Lord from this day forward. Guide my life and help me to do Your will. I receive You into my life as my Savior and I choose to follow You and serve You all my life. Thank You for hearing my prayer, I pray this in the name of Jesus, Amen.

If you prayed this prayer, please send me an email at booking@karabarker.net. I'd love to celebrate your new beginning with you. Accepting Jesus Christ and being saved is amazing and it is the best thing that can ever happen to you. It deserves to be celebrated. You might be afraid of getting baptized but don't let it scare you. I know it can be frightening but it's all going to be OK. Baptism is a public expression to everyone what Jesus has done inside of you and it's pretty awesome! After you've been baptized the next step is finding a church home and a mentor to help walk you through this new life. It doesn't have to be the wisest person in the world and it doesn't even have to be a pastor. I've had mentors that were not pastors at a church and they guided me to take steps I never could have done alone. It's just finding the right person, someone you look up to and that has the influence to speak into your life and help you grow in Christ.

· · · · · · · · · · · · · · · · · · · · · · · · · · · · · · · · · · · · · · · · · · · · · · · · · ·

· · · · · · · · · · · · · · · · · · · · · · · · · · · · · · · · · · · · · · · · · · · · · · · · · ·

· · · · · · · · · · · · · · · · · · · · · · · · · · · · · · · · · · · · · · · · · · · · · · · · · ·

· · · · · · · · · · · · · · · · · · · · · · · · · · · · · · · · · · · · · · · · · · · · · · · · · ·

· · · · · · · · · · · · · · · · · · · · · · · · · · · · · · · · · · · · · · · · · · · · · · · · · ·

· · · · · · · · · · · · · · · · · · · · · · · · · · · · · · · · · · · · · · · · · · · · · · · · · ·

· · · · · · · · · · · · · · · · · · · · · · · · · · · · · · · · · · · · · · · · · · · · · · · · · ·

## Prayer for Today

Heavenly Father, with every breath I take I feel Your power in me. I am thankful for the gift of life and for the body of Christ, the church. Lord, I ask that You open the eyes of my heart so that I may live righteously as You've taught us in Your word. May I be empowered by your Holy Spirit to keep spreading your Gospel. May Your mercy on me save me from the temptations of the world. I will eternally praise Your name. In Jesus' name, Amen.

# DAY 94
## Sprinkles of Joy

I will thank the Lord with all my heart! I will tell about all your amazing deeds! I will be happy and rejoice in you! I will sing praises to you, O sovereign One!

**– PSALM 9:1-2 NET**

Who doesn't want to feel complete joy and bliss in life? Everyone is looking for joy. Marketing companies know this. Every commercial promises the same outcome from their product: joy. Want some joy? Buy our ice cream. Want some joy? Sleep on this mattress. Want some joy? Buy this property, drive this car, wear this dress. Every commercial portrays the image of a joy-filled person. But what they are selling is what I call contingent joy. What God provides is contagious joy, the joy you experience when you encounter the grace, love and mercy of God. Joy is a funny thing. When it's taken from you, it's gone, but when it's willingly given, it multiplies. If we seek to hold on to our joy and hoard it all to ourselves, it soon becomes stale, but if we look for places to share and express it, it becomes much more than what we originally had. I think joy is feeling God's pleasure. So many people think joy is experiencing their own pleasure. But it doesn't work like that. When we bring joy and delight to the heart of God, He lets us know that deep down inside us, and our heart smiles. When Jesus sent the larger group of His disciples out to minister in His name for the first time, they returned full of excited stories of what had happened. They also "returned with joy" (Luke 10:17). "Jesus, full of joy through the Holy Spirit, said, 'I praise you, Father, Lord of heaven and earth, because you have hidden these things from the wise and learned, and revealed them to little children. Yes, Father, for this was your good pleasure'" (Luke 10:21). When we are doing the Father's good pleasure, the things He has called and gifted us to do, His joy is transferred to our hearts, strengthening us to please Him. After all, "the joy of the Lord is your strength" (Nehemiah 8:10). When Olympic sprinter Eric Liddell ran, he experienced the joy of God. "God made me fast, and when I run, I feel His pleasure," he said. One way for us to practice thankfulness and joy in our God is by reading the Psalms. Our happiness is found in what God has done for us. Our rejoicing is found in who our God is. There will be painful moments. There will be tough days. There will be times where our hearts are breaking and heavy. But we have a permanent joy that cannot be stolen because our joy is rooted in who God is and what He has done for us through Jesus.

Because God's love for us is perfect and because our God never changes we have the ability to have joy and contentment in any and all circumstances.

· · · · · · · · · · · · · · · · · · · · · · · · · · · · · · · · · · · · · · · · · · · · · · · · · · · ·

· · · · · · · · · · · · · · · · · · · · · · · · · · · · · · · · · · · · · · · · · · · · · · · · · · · ·

· · · · · · · · · · · · · · · · · · · · · · · · · · · · · · · · · · · · · · · · · · · · · · · · · · · ·

· · · · · · · · · · · · · · · · · · · · · · · · · · · · · · · · · · · · · · · · · · · · · · · · · · · ·

· · · · · · · · · · · · · · · · · · · · · · · · · · · · · · · · · · · · · · · · · · · · · · · · · · · ·

· · · · · · · · · · · · · · · · · · · · · · · · · · · · · · · · · · · · · · · · · · · · · · · · · · · ·

· · · · · · · · · · · · · · · · · · · · · · · · · · · · · · · · · · · · · · · · · · · · · · · · · · · ·

## *Prayer for Today*

Heavenly Father, You are my strength and my redeemer. You are my healer and my provider. Lord, I give all my worries and cares to You. I lay it all at Your feet. Fill me with Your joy and take away my sadness. In Jesus' name, Amen.

# *Nurture Yourself*

If I then, your Lord and Teacher, have washed your feet, you also ought to wash one another's feet.
For I have given you an example, that you also should do just as I have done to you."
**– JOHN 13:14-15 ESV**

No one can nurture like a mother. Sure men can care for others too, but not with the same touch a mother has. Nurturing is a gift of feminine nature tucked deep within our hearts by God. Who do children run to when they are hurt, sick, or hungry? Mom. We care. We love. We provide. We encourage. We nurture. Mothers provide the gentle caress that all lives need and even long for. We live in an interesting world that knows what it means to choose nurture. Think about it, behind every living thing is someone giving it life. All day long we tend to our busy schedules, demanding careers, relationships that require attention, time and energy. It didn't take until I was about 40 years old to learn this life lesson that there is a difference between things that serve only to fill up my time and the things that serve to fill me up, enough that I have something to pour into the areas of my life that I truly care to do right by: My family, my relationships, and the work that keeps me flat-footed and planted.

A few years ago, I found myself in a dark place of stress and self-induced anxiety. Unbalanced by how much I was pouring out without being poured into in the ways I desperately needed. I learned that eventually the well would run dry because I was constantly double seeping my pail to get out water for everyone else except myself. So I had to shift my mindset by denouncing the idea that busy meant being productive and started to move some things off of my plate and add things that mattered that promoted growth and spiritual renewal. I had to start creating space to nurture what fills my cup so I would have the desire and energy to give my best to the things in my life that I wanted to thrive in. Don't allow the world to cause you to deny what you know to be true. It is why we feel for others like we do, it is why we care for people we don't even know. It is the longing inside of us to help the hurting, to fix the broken and to care for the neglected. It is a Christ-like call upon your life. Listen to it and cherish it.

. . . . . . . . . . . . . . . . . . . . . . . . . . . . . . . . . . . . . . . . . . . . . . . . . . . . . . . . . . . . . . .

. . . . . . . . . . . . . . . . . . . . . . . . . . . . . . . . . . . . . . . . . . . . . . . . . . . . . . . . . . . . . . .

. . . . . . . . . . . . . . . . . . . . . . . . . . . . . . . . . . . . . . . . . . . . . . . . . . . . . . . . . . . . . . .

. . . . . . . . . . . . . . . . . . . . . . . . . . . . . . . . . . . . . . . . . . . . . . . . . . . . . . . . . . . . . . .

. . . . . . . . . . . . . . . . . . . . . . . . . . . . . . . . . . . . . . . . . . . . . . . . . . . . . . . . . . . . . . .

. . . . . . . . . . . . . . . . . . . . . . . . . . . . . . . . . . . . . . . . . . . . . . . . . . . . . . . . . . . . . . .

## Prayer for Today

Loving God, You have commanded us to show mercy and compassion to one another. I come to You for help because I believe You always provide what we need to accomplish Your will. With so much at stake in this lost and hurting world, Lord, I pray that You please give me a heart that is compassionate and merciful towards others. In Jesus' name, Amen.

# DAY 96

## Ready or Not

Devote yourselves to prayer, keeping alert in it with an attitude of thanksgiving;
**– COLOSSIANS 4:2 NIV**

In 2021, my husband and I took a bucket list trip to East Africa and went on a safari in Kenya, toured the beautiful beaches in Seychelles Islands and retreated to a boutique mansion in the mountains of Kampala, Uganda for 21 days. This was a trip of a lifetime and I literally started packing 30 days prior to our departure. I had a master list of things to get done while trying to stay healthy and fit so I could look amazing in the light linen clothing during the trip.

Women are great at preparing and getting ready for things, especially getaways. From parties to trips, we are the best planners. Some events are easy and take a short time to prepare. Others, like weddings and babies, take several months or even years of preparation. We carefully plan so when the big moment arrives we are set. However, I find it interesting that while people are good at preparing for earthly events we often totally neglect the eternal ones. When it comes to where we will spend our afterlife, we put it off. Shoving it to the back of the pantry like that can of tomato paste we know we will need eventually. We will "get right with God" when the time comes. Maybe when we get a terminal diagnosis or when we are really old. It is hard to worry about the end of life when we are so busy just living life in the now. Does it really matter that much?

Let me tell you, it matters. And it matters right now. You are not guaranteed another second let alone another day, year or decade. God's Word reminds us of this frequently with verses such as: "yet you do not know what tomorrow will bring. What is your life? For you are a mist that appears for a little time and then vanishes." (James 4:14). Our lives go by in a flash, especially when compared to eternity. Let's be serious. We may think we have years ahead but we may only have seconds. Get ready.

We are told in Hebrews 9:27 that it is appointed for man to die once, and after that comes judgment. In the blink of an eye you could be standing before your Maker. By then your fate is sealed. There is no trial, no arguments to be had, no "Wait God, I can explain." No comparing yourself to the person in the pew next to you, they won't be there. Only you, God and a just and final judgment. Either the blood of Jesus Christ will mark you as His or it won't. Either debt paid in full or debt fully due. If you show up on your wedding day without a dress you can still get married. If the baby comes before you have purchased a crib, you still get the baby. But if you die before accepting Jesus as Lord and Savior, you are forever damned. The choice has to be made now. Do not wait. Purgatory is a lie. Do not find false security in a make-believe destination. Jesus is the only way to the Father. Read it all for yourself in God's Word, a book written so that you would read it and know. No paid clergy needed to filter the truth for you. God is real. "The fool says in his heart, 'There is no God.'" (Psalms 14:1). Do not be a fool. Each of us deep within senses the truth of this. We long to worship something and we long for a purpose for our existence. We long to be loved and to be part of a family. This is because the truth is written on our hearts (Romans 2:15). Do not ignore the hanging question any longer. Will you repent and turn from your sin and believe in Jesus Christ the Son of God? If you call yourself a Christian, but you live a continuous lifestyle of sin, you're not prepared. You are either standing in grace at this moment, having accepted the sacrifice of Jesus on your behalf, or you are standing under God's wrath and condemnation, having rejected Him and preferring to pay for your own sins for eternity (see John 3:18). It is up to you, and don't just jump to Day 97 in the journal. This is too important to be straddling the fence. Either you're ready or not. Seek out the truth today, why not?

. . . . . . . . . . . . . . . . . . . . . . . . . . . . . . . . . . . . . . . . . . . . . . . . . . . . . . . . . . . . .

. . . . . . . . . . . . . . . . . . . . . . . . . . . . . . . . . . . . . . . . . . . . . . . . . . . . . . . . . . . . .

. . . . . . . . . . . . . . . . . . . . . . . . . . . . . . . . . . . . . . . . . . . . . . . . . . . . . . . . . . . . .

. . . . . . . . . . . . . . . . . . . . . . . . . . . . . . . . . . . . . . . . . . . . . . . . . . . . . . . . . . . . .

. . . . . . . . . . . . . . . . . . . . . . . . . . . . . . . . . . . . . . . . . . . . . . . . . . . . . . . . . . . . .

. . . . . . . . . . . . . . . . . . . . . . . . . . . . . . . . . . . . . . . . . . . . . . . . . . . . . . . . . . . . .

. . . . . . . . . . . . . . . . . . . . . . . . . . . . . . . . . . . . . . . . . . . . . . . . . . . . . . . . . . . . .

## Prayer for Today

Dear Father God, I pray that You will help me have a heart of readiness. May I be ready to respond to You whenever You call and for whatever You ask of me. I choose to be available for Your service and pray that I will be obedient to You on a daily basis. May my response to You be immediate! No questions, no hesitation, and no excuses! I come to follow You Lord! Amen.

# The Waiting Room

For promotion and power come from nowhere on earth, but only from God. He promotes one and deposes another.

**—PSALM 75:6-7 TLB**

Waiting on God. This can be one of the most challenging aspects of the Christian walk. Perhaps you know that there's a destiny in your life and want it to go ahead and start already, or maybe you're hungry to be influential and are seeking out opportunities to lead. The waiting season is important but it's one that most people want to avoid, thinking that it's boring or painful. But what if we realized that the Lord is not a distant God who is withholding good things from us? What if we shifted our perspective from seeing waiting as withholding but rather as preparation? When I think of waiting, I think of a good Father who wants to pull me in close and teach me His ways. I think of God's protection. Did you ever think that waiting might just be the best thing for you, and the people around you? So why do people get prematurely promoted? I think one side of the coin is that people don't know the timing or season God has them in, so they jump ahead before they're properly prepared. However, another side of the coin has to do with the people who promote others before the time is right. Did you know that if you try to bypass your waiting season and try to elevate yourself before you're ready, you could actually delay your blessing? Between the promise and the palace there should always be a process. One that is natural and needed. It is the process that prepares and develops us so that we have the character it takes and the skills necessary to be successful in the palace. We all need the process of preparation before the promotion.

. . . . . . . . . . . . . . . . . . . . . . . . . . . . . . . . . . . . . . . . . . . . . . . . . . . . . . . . . . . . . . .

. . . . . . . . . . . . . . . . . . . . . . . . . . . . . . . . . . . . . . . . . . . . . . . . . . . . . . . . . . . . . . .

. . . . . . . . . . . . . . . . . . . . . . . . . . . . . . . . . . . . . . . . . . . . . . . . . . . . . . . . . . . . . . .

. . . . . . . . . . . . . . . . . . . . . . . . . . . . . . . . . . . . . . . . . . . . . . . . . . . . . . . . . . . . . . .

. . . . . . . . . . . . . . . . . . . . . . . . . . . . . . . . . . . . . . . . . . . . . . . . . . . . . . . . . . . . . . .

. . . . . . . . . . . . . . . . . . . . . . . . . . . . . . . . . . . . . . . . . . . . . . . . . . . . . . . . . . . . . . .

. . . . . . . . . . . . . . . . . . . . . . . . . . . . . . . . . . . . . . . . . . . . . . . . . . . . . . . . . . . . . . .

## Prayer for Today

Heavenly Father, I wait earnestly for the promotion that is facilitated by You alone. Let your presence command blessings into my life in Jesus' name. Amen.

# DAY 98
## FitBit Faith

For a day in your courts is better than a thousand elsewhere. I would rather be a doorkeeper in the house of my God than dwell in the tents of wickedness.
**— PSALM 84:10 ESV**

How hard do you work at being Christ-like? Do you take it as seriously as staying healthy, earning money, working out, managing a home or pursuing your favorite hobbies? I struggle in this area and I think many other women do too. We often treat this Christian life as lackadaisical. We're all too willing to play a passive role as we attend church and just hope God will gently change our ways eventually. Slowly.......becoming....... more.......like.......Jesus.

Was this the lifestyle God had in mind for Christians when He had Paul write in Philippians 3:12-14: "Not that I have already obtained this or am already perfect, but I press on to make it my own, because Christ Jesus has made me his own. Brothers, one thing I do: forgetting what lies behind and straining forward to what lies ahead, I press on toward the goal for the prize of the upward call of God in Christ Jesus." Yeah, I don't think so. Nothing about this passage sounds passive to me. Neither did Paul display passivity in his life in working toward obedience to Christ. Several years ago, my husband bought me a FitBit device. I didn't even know I wanted one until he gave me one. I also don't remember ever caring how many steps I took in a 24 hour period until I started using it. I set a goal of getting 15,000 steps in per day and I'm really working at it. Often, I find myself looking down at my wrist to see how many steps I have taken and how many I have yet to go (usually lots). I'm taking walks and hopping on the treadmill. Why? What has changed? A goal has been set. Let me ask you something today. If you knew that 15,000 steps would get you closer to Jesus, how hard would you work to take those steps? How much of your time would be devoted to that one goal of being close to Him? For those of us who are His, there is no greater prize than to be with Jesus. My hope is that we would run hard and "strain forward to what lies ahead" like Paul. Friends, we need to work hard at being more like Christ because Christ has made us His own. We have an upward call upon our lives. A directive to move toward God in Christ. We should break a sweat as we slay sin in our lives and move toward holiness. Expend the energy necessary because every step counts and every step is worth it. Trust me, Christ is worth the pursuit. So, arm yourself with His word and take the next step, today!

. . . . . . . . . . . . . . . . . . . . . . . . . . . . . . . . . . . . . . . . . . . . . . . . . . . . . . . .

. . . . . . . . . . . . . . . . . . . . . . . . . . . . . . . . . . . . . . . . . . . . . . . . . . . . . . . .

. . . . . . . . . . . . . . . . . . . . . . . . . . . . . . . . . . . . . . . . . . . . . . . . . . . . . . . .

. . . . . . . . . . . . . . . . . . . . . . . . . . . . . . . . . . . . . . . . . . . . . . . . . . . . . . . .

. . . . . . . . . . . . . . . . . . . . . . . . . . . . . . . . . . . . . . . . . . . . . . . . . . . . . . . .

. . . . . . . . . . . . . . . . . . . . . . . . . . . . . . . . . . . . . . . . . . . . . . . . . . . . . . . .

. . . . . . . . . . . . . . . . . . . . . . . . . . . . . . . . . . . . . . . . . . . . . . . . . . . . . . . .

## *Prayer for Today*

Give me that boldness, Lord God. Let me be a strong warrior for You and in my life. Push me through my fear to the other side, to the Promised Land with my name on it. Propel me into the face of my fear and right through it, to Your destiny for my life. In Jesus' name, Amen.

# Girl, Read Your Bible

Therefore I, the prisoner in the Lord, urge you to walk worthy of the calling you have received, with all humility and gentleness, with patience, bearing with one another in love, making every effort to keep the unity of the Spirit through the bond of peace. There is one body and one Spirit—just as you were called to one hope at your calling—one Lord, one faith, one baptism, one God and Father of all, who is above all and through all and in all.

**—EPHESIANS 4:1–6**

The Bible is life-changing. Not only does reading and responding to God's Word change our lives today, it can continue to change our lives as we keep coming back to it over and over throughout our lifetime. It's not enough just to have the Word, but we need to incorporate it into our daily lives to keep coming back to the Word. I believe in prayer but if you neglect getting into the Word of God through reading the Bible you are missing out on receiving God's full power. The power that belongs to God is stored up in the great reservoir of His own Word, the Bible. We cannot obtain or maintain God's power in our own lives or in our work unless there is deep and frequent meditation on His Word. If you are lost and need direction you would likely stop and ask someone familiar with that area to help direct you. Well let's face it, nobody knows the Word better than the Author Himself. Before you open your bible, begin with a simple prayer asking God to direct your time and focus in His word to reap the greatest blessing and for His glory. When you pray, simply quiet your mind as much as you can and begin to notice the whispers and small voices you sense. Many times when I begin my study time like this I'll hear the Lord speak a book of the Bible or the name of a person in His word. Other times it's quiet. If that's the case, don't worry, when you invite the Holy Spirit to direct your time in the Word, you can rest assured it is in competent hands and nothing you read, study or pray will ever be meaningless or without purpose.

God's word NEVER returns void and it will always accomplish His purposes. So, even if you don't understand the reason for what you read at the moment, many times you will experience an "ah-ha" moment later that day, week or months down the road that helps you recognize Him at work in your life!

*Day*

# 99

· · · · · · · · · · · · · · · · · · · · · · · · · · · · · · · · · · · · · · · · · · · · · ·

· · · · · · · · · · · · · · · · · · · · · · · · · · · · · · · · · · · · · · · · · · · · · ·

· · · · · · · · · · · · · · · · · · · · · · · · · · · · · · · · · · · · · · · · · · · · · ·

· · · · · · · · · · · · · · · · · · · · · · · · · · · · · · · · · · · · · · · · · · · · · ·

· · · · · · · · · · · · · · · · · · · · · · · · · · · · · · · · · · · · · · · · · · · · · ·

· · · · · · · · · · · · · · · · · · · · · · · · · · · · · · · · · · · · · · · · · · · · · · · ·

· · · · · · · · · · · · · · · · · · · · · · · · · · · · · · · · · · · · · · · · · · ·

## Prayer for Today

Lord Jesus, Father God, Holy Spirit I thank You for giving me a guidebook and a road map for how to do life through your Word. I thank You that it is alive and vibrant and timely. I thank You that through it You speak directly into my life, provide wisdom, inspire change and refresh my soul. Lord, as I open Your Word today, I do so expectantly and with gratitude. I ask You now to take the wheel and direct this time spent with You. Will You help me to hear You and will You guide and direct me to exactly the words and messages I need to hear from You today that will produce the greatest blessings for me and those around me and bring You the most glory. I thank You in advance for revealing Yourself to me through Your Word. In Jesus' name, Amen.

# Breakthroughs Are Coming

"See, I am doing a new thing! Now it springs up; do you not perceive it? I am making a way in the wilderness and streams in the wasteland."

**—ISAIAH 43:19 NIV**

Have you ever trusted God for a breakthrough but were still surprised when a miracle actually happened? How is it that we can say we believe God for something but at the same time, we're not truly expecting anything to happen? Well, it is Day 100 and I declare your sudden breakthrough is here! I like the word "suddenly." God is the God of "suddenly." In fact, did you know that "suddenly" appears in the Bible 87 times. That doesn't count words like behold, immediately or unexpectedly, which have the same meaning as "suddenly." "Suddenly" is not just for biblical times or biblical characters, it's for you and I too. I applaud you for your commitment and dedication to reading 100 days of these God-inspired devotional stories with prayers. I believe God will honor your commitment and faithfulness to stick it out with me. 100 days is over a quarter of the year, so I pray that this time was not vain but you experienced several suddenly's along this journey with me. I recall several instances where the word suddenly was used in the Bible. The angel "suddenly" appeared to Mary and gave her "sudden" news. "Suddenly" a great host of angels appeared around the shepherds at Jesus' birth. "Suddenly" an angel appeared inside Jesus' empty tomb. "Suddenly" Jesus appeared to two men walking on a road called Damascus. The Bible says that Jesus will "suddenly" return when no one expects it. Whether you're in a valley, like David, fear will try to occupy that valley. In the morning, anxiety will try to come into that valley. At night, before you go to bed, stress, doubt and intimidation will try to keep you up at night. But know this; that valley doesn't belong to the enemy. It belongs to praise. Now you've got to take your valley back. All through the day when the thoughts come saying, "It's not going to work out. The problem is never going to turn around," don't dwell on that. Don't let that occupy that valley. Turn up your praise and begin proclaiming, "Father, thank You that You are still on the throne. Thank You that You are bigger than this obstacle. Thank You for fighting my battles. Thank You for the answer that is already on the way." When you learn to give God praise in the valley, you will begin defeating the many giants of life. It doesn't matter how big that obstacle is. You and God are a majority. He will always cause you to triumph. Praise causes God to go to work that will lead to your breakthrough. Praise breaks the chains that are holding you back. Praise opens up supernatural doors and new opportunities. Praise causes things to fall back into place. You have prayed about the situation long enough, it is time to switch over into praise because your breakthrough is on the way! If you'll dig your heels in and offer up a sacrifice of praise, God promises He is going to reverse and restore. Like Abraham, you will see the dream come to pass. Like David, you will defeat your giant. Like Elijah, the drought will come to an end. I believe and declare; you will see the abundance of rain, abundance of joy, abundance in your health, abundance in your finances, abundance of God's goodness. Your breakthrough is on the horizon and by faith I hope you will experience a suddenly moment because of your commitment. This is your season of unexpected, unbelievable, unfathomable, unshakeable and unimaginable breakthroughs! In Jesus' Name! Amen and Amen.

. . . . . . . . . . . . . . . . . . . . . . . . . . . . . . . . . . . . . . . . . . . . . . . . .

. . . . . . . . . . . . . . . . . . . . . . . . . . . . . . . . . . . . . . . . . . . . . . . . .

. . . . . . . . . . . . . . . . . . . . . . . . . . . . . . . . . . . . . . . . . . . . . . . . .

. . . . . . . . . . . . . . . . . . . . . . . . . . . . . . . . . . . . . . . . . . . . . . . . .

. . . . . . . . . . . . . . . . . . . . . . . . . . . . . . . . . . . . . . . . . . . . . . . . .

. . . . . . . . . . . . . . . . . . . . . . . . . . . . . . . . . . . . . . . . . . . . . . . . .

## *Prayer for Today*

Heavenly Father, thank You for the breakthrough that is about to come over my situation. I will press on until I see Your promise come to pass in my life. I won't allow the enemy to play tricks on my mind for I have the mind of Christ and I know that in all things, Christ has already given me victory even in this situation of my life. So I command the heavenly host of angels to capture all demons assigned in my life, in my family, in my city, in my nation and in all things that matter to me! Thank You God for I know that You will never leave me nor forsake me. I am safe and secure in Your hands and You have given me the peace that crushes satan under my feet. Thank You God for breakthrough in Jesus' mighty name, Amen!

## Adios, Ciao and Goodbyes

This book is dedicated to Bear. You are the jelly to my peanut butter. You are the smile to my face. You are the gravy to my mashed potatoes. You are the bubbles to my bath. You are the icing to my cupcake. The spring to my step. The water to my ocean. The best to my friend. The love of my life. Thank you for always being there to give me squeeze hugs.

To my three kids, Marika, Maiya and Micah. Because of you three, I am a Mommy to some amazing beings on earth.